# Angels
## or
# Virtual Visions

*Patrick A. Koneval*

Copyright © 2016 by Patrick A. Koneval

All Rights Reserved. No part of this book may be
reproduced, stored in a retrieval system, or transmitted,
in any form or by any means, electronic, mechanical,
photocopying, recording, or otherwise, without the prior
written permission of the author.

Printed in the United States of America.

Published by PASK Publishing

ISBN: 978-0-692-81450-5

Visit us at www.angelsorvirtualvisions.com

## Acknowledgements

There are so many people I need to thank for helping make this book go from a simple dream to reality. I would like to first thank God for helping me find the words. There were many times I asked for help. It has been a two-year process with many long days. I would also like to thank my wife Sandy, and my two kids, Brenden and Samantha. Their love, support, and time allowed me to slip away and write. I will be forever grateful. You mean the world to me! Jennifer Trice, Bonnie Gibson, and Glenn Rexer, without your help, guidance, and wisdom, this book would have never been published. To the rest of my family, friends, colleagues, and students, may God bless you all!

# CONTENTS

## INTRODUCTION

Father Smith always had a way of taking the sermon and applying it to our everyday life. Today was no different. He was talking about learning to accept help and how anything was possible through or with God.

"My brothers and sisters, it is ok to ask for help once in a while. We all do it, but we should learn to do it more. You are not a lesser man or woman because you asked for help. Your pride is not challenged! The Bible says that those who exalt themselves will be brought down while those who humble themselves will be raised up by God."

He continued to talk about how we all face challenges that become somewhat tolerable when we have the help and support of others. Then, he added how anything was possible through or with God.

"This reminds me of a story. It is about Elijah and the horses. He was sent to tell King Ahab that the three-year drought would be over. He went to the top of Mount Carmel and saw a cloud form over the sea. He then proceeded to run from Mount Carmel to Jezreel. It was about twenty miles. In the process, he outran the horses and chariots. A man outran horses! How? How did he do that? He had the help of God. That's how! Anything is possible when we have God's help."

I began to wonder how this was possible. Could that really happen? After mass, we headed home, and I went to finish some schoolwork. What happened next shocked even me! As I was sitting at my computer, I felt as though someone was in the room with me, so I slowly turned around.

"My name is Andrew, and I am an angel.

I could not believe what I was hearing. So, I repeated what he had said.

"Are you really an angel? If so, how did you get here? What do you want? Why are you showing yourself to me?"

"These are all great questions, Daniel, and I promise I will answer everyone one of them, but for now, let's just take everything very slowly."

I was not sure what he meant by slowly, but I would do my best to comply with what he was asking.

"How many times have you prayed and asked for help? How many times have you said you just wanted to have a conversation with God? How many times have you said that you wished God was as present today as He was in the Old Testament? I am here for those reasons!"

I was stunned and didn't know what to say. How do you answer something like that? I am sure other people pray and ask the same questions I do. Why was I the chosen one? Why was I so special?

Andrew continued to talk. "Everyone on this earth has a purpose, and you have wondered what your purpose has been for a very long time. I am here to help you with that, and when we are done, you need to promise me something."

"What?" I exclaimed!

"You need to write about everything we are talking about, and everything that is going to happen to you."

"But, I am not a writer," I said.

"That does not matter. It is not how you write, but more importantly what you write," he stated. "Promise me!"

"Ok, I promise," I said.

"Good!  Now, we can get started," he said.

Andrew began by telling me that I was as stubborn as a mule, but my heart was in the right place.

"I apologize about my language.  Angels don't normally talk like that, but, it really does fit.  We have been watching you for a long time.  We have been watching everyone for a long time.  Every person on earth has a guardian angel that stays with them from birth until they come home," he said.

"Does this mean you will tell me about heaven?  God?  Angels?"

"All in due time, my friend.  I will answer as many questions as you would like.  However, let me warn you.  You will be judged, and many people may not believe you, but this is where being so stubborn may help you."

I guess I should not have been so shocked.  I have read numerous books on God, Jesus, and Angels and was completely fascinated.  I was also very interested in any movie with this sort of theme.  My basement had different pictures of Jesus.  I always liked to tease my wife and tell her that He would watch over me while I worked out. If I could sit down and have a conversation with one person, it would be Him.

Andrew was right! I talked to God often throughout the day and asked Him to help guide me with certain decisions. I often asked why I did not hear from Him.

Andrew stared at me, and I felt as though his gaze went right to my soul and said, "We will see if we can fix that hole in your heart. I know it has been there for quite a long time, so I need to give you your homework assignments," he continued.

"I have homework!" I exclaimed.

"Yes, you do! You need to do two things. First, you need to start to let people know about your life and how you got to this point. Write it down like you would if you were writing a book. Make chapters and describe events that were significant. We need to give people a background so they understand why this is happening. Start with the beginning and stop when you reach our conversation. Second, you need to get yourself in the absolute best shape possible. You have no idea what is coming, but it has something to do with your brain research. Talk about that as well. I will be back in about three months."

"Ok, Andrew, I will get it done. Do I tell my wife about you and our conversations?"

"Doesn't your wife know about your angel fascinations? I think she does, and I know she will be supportive, but to answer your question, yes, please tell your wife everything. You will need her love and support down the road."

"Ok, I will do that as soon as we finish."

"And, Daniel"

"Yes, Andrew?"

"I hope you are ready because you have no idea what is about to happen. Nooooo idea!"

With that he disappeared, and I sat down to begin putting everything down on paper like I was asked to do.

## CHAPTER 1

I was a quiet kid growing up and did not have a ton of friends, so I turned to sports. I picked up my first baseball, basketball, and football at age one and never really put them down after that. I was a pretty good player in all three, but basketball was my true love.

I continued to play all three sports, but in eighth grade I got my second concussion playing football, and my career was over. It was an innocent enough play. I was the quarterback, and we were scrimmaging the ninth grade. We had just got a first down, and the ninth grade coach was angry. He hollered at his players and told them, "I promise you, if they get one more yard, you will all run the rest of practice." Boy, did they take his directions to heart because the very next play, I was crushed. I had no idea where I was. Somehow, I made it to the locker room, and the coach told me to stay where I was while he called my parents. Of course, I left, and my father found me wandering the sub.

Ninth grade was a great year for me, but also a turning point in my life. I played very well and hit my first solid home run in baseball. It was your typical bottom of the

7th, two on and two outs. I was down to my last strike and knew I was going to get a fast ball. It was a little high, but I sent it over the left fielder's head. It was an awesome feeling!

I was lucky enough to play basketball in two different leagues during my ninth grade year. Once the first league was over, I played for my school. I had a few 30 point games and started to get a name for myself. In one specific game, we had seven seconds left on the clock. I took the ball out of bounds and passed it to one of my teammates named Bob. He passed it right back, and I took the ball the length of the court, squared up, and took the shot. It went in, and we won the game.

After basketball season was over, I was starting to get some interest from some private schools. One school was so interested in me; they had another guard come with them for my meeting. They explained to me their plan and said the two of us would take them to the state championship. I was very interested and asked if I could wait until after camp to give my answer. Camp was great! When I first arrived, I could just smell basketball. We were taken to our dorm rooms and asked to come to the gym for a short introductory meeting. There were a lot of kids, and some really talented ball players. Camp was run by a Division I coach, and was at a Division I school. Each day we would get up and eat, have about an hour to get to the gym, and start our drills. After drills we played our games and had our contests.

I was doing very well and was invited to play with the college guys at night, once the day camp was over. What a feeling it was to be on the court with college players! They were so good it was scary, but I held my own. On the last day of camp, I was practicing my free throws. I had shot 96% during the week, and I was approached by the coach who ran the camp. He told me I was the best natural shooter he had ever seen and wanted to offer me a college scholarship. Little did I know that my decision would change the entire course of my life.

After returning home from camp, I had visits from more schools. They were pressuring me to make up my mind and decide where I was going to go. I sat down and talked to my parents about what they thought I should do. They told me it was my decision, and would support me in any way they could. On the night before I was going to announce where I was going to go, I received a phone call from my local high school coach. He was the

JV coach, and he asked me if he could come to my house since he was in the area.

Once the coach rang my bell, he introduced himself.

"Hello, Daniel! My name is Roy Parker, and I would like to talk to you about your basketball future."

"Sure, come on in," I said.

"I know you have had several schools interested in you and they want you to go to their school, but the best place for you is our school. First, they are an all boys' school, and I don't think you would like that. Won't you miss all your friends? Second, you will start every game and move up to the varsity by midyear. Last, we will turn you into the biggest star this school has ever seen, and you will play division I basketball when you are done here."

I was a little shocked by this bold statement.

"How can I be sure you can deliver on all of this?" "I have been coaching a long time and so has the varsity coach. We know what we are doing. We know talent when we see it," he said.

It all sounded good to me, but what did I know? I was only 15 years old. I asked if I could have the night to make my decision, and he said, "Take all the time you need. Just call me one way or the other."

I decided to go to my local high school and give up going to the private schools. I thought of what it would be like to play on the varsity team midyear and really start to get some other colleges to take a look at me. I continued to work my butt off until school started. I would do whatever needed to be done to get ahead.

My coach called early on a Friday and told me we would have a scrimmage against a very tough city team. I knew the competition would be fierce, but I was totally excited about it. I mentally prepared myself for the tough physical play and stepped onto the court. We all shook hands, and the ball was tossed up. We were underway!

Unfortunately, our starting center hurt his knee a few minutes into the second quarter. Both the varsity coach, junior varsity coach, and our trainer took Tom to the locker room and left his father, Mr. Simmons in charge. A few minutes later, the other team had a fast break. It was a two on one, and I knew I was going to get nailed, but took the charge anyway. The ref blew the whistle.

"Charging! One in one," he said.

I stood up with both a bloody lip and bloody nose and started to walk to the free throw line.

"Lavenok out, Vertamule in!" Mr. Simmons screamed.

"Sure Mr. Simmons. Can I just shoot my free throws first?"

I was not sure he knew I had a one in one.

"Now Lavenok or you will be cut from this team," he said. Boy, was I angry. I slammed the ball on the floor and walked off the court. After the coaches came back, Mr. Simmons told them I had an attitude and needed to be taught a lesson.

I was taught a lesson, and the coach benched me for the first eight games of the season. I was so frustrated that I wanted to quit. I talked to my father about this, and he told me I would regret it.

"He has to play you. He cannot afford to keep you out any longer. Your team is losing, and he has to do something to change so you can start winning," he said.

I was not so sure, but my father was right. I started all the remaining games of the season and averaged over 20 points a game. I played very well! After the season, I talked to one of the coaches from the private school that had talked to me. My spot was given away. I was stuck!

I went to all the team camps over the summer and even gave up my family vacation. The coach said if we did not go, we would not be able to play on the team this season. He liked to create an atmosphere of competition. He did not know how to coach, and I was learning this more and more each week. My major downfall came one day at summer practice. I was practicing my three-point shooting when I heard the coach call my name.

"Hey Lavenok? How about a friendly game of star?"

"Sure coach," I said. "Who goes first?"

"I am the coach, so I will go first. You know, Lavenok, I have been coaching for over twenty years and have never lost. I expect that streak to continue."

When someone challenges me, I have this switch that sometimes goes off. It is hard to explain, but I feel something inside of me change. It is like I lose sight of everything around me and focus totally on the challenge that is before me. I took his words to heart and set out to be the first person to beat Coach Misty.

He did pretty well, but shooting was my specialty, and I beat him. Oh man, he was not a happy guy, and stormed off the court. Many of the players came up to me and told me that I was stupid to beat him. I did not know any better. I thought he challenged me to a game, and the best man would win.

Well, I found out my teammates were right. After basketball tryouts, I was called into the coach's office.

"Lavenok, I am sorry, but I just don't have enough uniforms this year to keep you,"

"You are kidding right," I stated.

"No, I am not kidding. Thanks for trying out."

At that, he turned and opened the door, and I left. I walked over to my locker and just sat on the bench trying to digest what had just happened. "How could I be cut," I thought? I was offered a scholarship to a division I school in 9th grade and was one of the best players in the state. Now, I was cut, and my basketball career was over my junior year. As one of the players walked by he said,

"Hey, Lavenok. You know why you were cut don't you. It was because you beat coach in the game. I heard him talking to Parker. Told you so!"

"Great," I thought. Now what am I going to do?

CHAPTER 2

The rest of high school was pretty tough for me, but there were a few bright moments. My all night party was one of those moments. A group of my friends and I decided to take on the varsity basketball team, and we beat them. There was no trash talking. We just went out and played. It was such a great feeling to be back on the court again, and it was even better to be playing with people that loved the game like I did.

I tried out for the baseball team, but since I did not play in tenth grade, the coach told all players at practice that day, thank you, but we don't need you. I ran track and was pretty good at it, but after my second meet my parents told me if I wanted to go to college, I needed to find a job to pay for it. Fortunately, or unfortunately, I was offered a great job through one of my friends doing landscaping. They were going to pay us very well and all in cash. I had no choice but to quit track one point shy of my varsity letter.

Once I graduated, my girlfriend and I got more serious. We planned on going to college together, but we were not sure what our major would be. About a week before classes started at the local community college, I received a call from my Jr. High principal. He and I got along pretty well while I was there, and I always told him if he ever needed anything, just feel free to call me.

Well the phone did ring.

"Hey, Lavenok, how ya doing? Getting ready to go to college?"

"Yes, I am. It is great to hear from you. How is everything?"

"Great, but I need a favor," he replied.

"Sure, how can I help?" I asked.

"I lost my football coach. He is doing a principal internship, and I need you to coach the team."

"May I get back to you on this?"

"Sure, just don't wait too long!"

"What the hell do I know about coaching a team?" I thought to myself. I was a good athlete, I knew sports, I played sports, but have never thought about coaching. I decided to call one of my friends and ask his advice. He told me just to share my knowledge with the players and try to break it down so they would understand.

I called my principal back and told him I would take the job. Another decision that changed my life! The season went well, and I learned an awful lot. After coaching that team, I told my girlfriend that I absolutely loved it and had decided to go into teaching. It was such a great feeling to build something out of nothing, to affect the lives of these students, that I figured I would do that the rest of my life.

My girlfriend enjoyed teaching as well, and we took classes together at the local community college. I was still missing basketball though and after a little convincing from my girlfriend, I decided to try out for the college team. I was excited to play again. When I walked into the gym and saw the basketballs lying around, it brought back memories of how much I loved the game. After changing and warming up, I stopped to take a look at my competition. I knew a lot of these guys from my playing days. I knew I had a pretty good chance of making the team, so I was excited when the coach blew the whistle and asked us all to circle up.

"My name is Coach Mitch. I am the head basketball coach here. These are open tryouts for our team. Before we get started, I need to ask one question. How many of you played basketball your senior year of high school?"

I saw about half the hands go up. Obviously, I did not put my hand up because I did not play, and I did not want to lie. That is just not me.

"Ok, if you have your hand up, please step over here."

"Awesome!" I thought. I will get a chance to show the coach I am every bit as good as the guys that played in high school.

"Ok, everyone that did not raise their hand, thank you for coming out, but we don't need you."

Just like in baseball, where I was not given a chance. My college tryout lasted a whole ten minutes. What a jerk this guy was! He did not even let me try out for the team. I figured I would just play parks and rec and try to enjoy myself.

During one of my classes, I met another student. His name was Hank Biamente.

"Hey, Lavenok? I saw you at practice the other day. Too bad Coach did not let you try out. I have seen you play."

"Yeah, well, it is what it is. He is a jerk anyway."

"I have a crazy idea," he said.

"Lay it on me."

"What if you and I formed our own team and took on the college team," he said with pure excitement.

"What?" I said.

"Listen, I need to tell you my story and then you will understand."

He proceeded to tell me that five years ago, the coach did the same thing to him that he did to me. He cut him in about ten minutes. Hank took a class here and there and, spent the next five years perfecting his game. Once he made the team, he told the coach where to go because he would not play for him.

"Hank, let me get this straight. You spent five years of your life working on your game to make the team so you could quit? Do I have this right?"

"Yep! I wanted to show the coach that I had what it took and teach him a lesson."

"Ok, Hank, I am in," I said.

After that, we went on the hunt to find the rest of our team.

It took about three weeks, but we found each of our players. One by one, Hank and I went to pick up games, practices, talked to people in class to find the right fit. Each guy would help our team in one way or another, but we also looked for the will to win. We looked for the guy that just would not quit. We weren't necessarily looking for the best players, but rather the right players. We began to practice and learn how to play together. I must say, I really enjoyed playing again. It was a great feeling! We started to get really good and ended up winning the parks and rec league. Once that was over, we decided to ask Coach Mitch if we could play the team. He thought it would be great practice for his guys and agreed to have us play.

Unfortunately for him, we absolutely destroyed the college team. It was not even close. We all played together. We played as a team. Many of the guys on the college team were from my high school and had the same attitude they did while in school. It was all about them. They played for themselves and were taught a great lesson of humility that day.

I also learned a lot from the whole experience. I learned to trust the guys I was playing with, but most importantly, I learned about hard work and how far someone would go for revenge. Hank was a great guy and a good friend. He had a goal in his head and set out to accomplish that goal. He let nothing get in his way, and he finally saw that goal come to fruition. It took five years, but he did it.

My girlfriend and I did well in college and graduated with honors. We both ended up getting a job where we did our student teaching. Life was going pretty well, and I decided to take the next step and ask my girlfriend to marry me. She said yes, and made me extremely happy.

We began to plan our wedding and look for an apartment. It was a lot of fun and very comforting to have someone know you so well be a part of your life. We got along great, and it was nice to have someone to share everything with.

After my first year of teaching, I was called into the principal's office. I asked what was going on.

"I am sorry Lavenok, but we have to lay you off. We have to lay off the last seven people we hired," my principal said.

"How do I tell my fiancé that I just lost my teaching job?" I said.

"I know, it is not fair, but that is teaching. You never know what is going to happen from year to year."

"Wow!" I thought. Everything was going so well and now this. Why does this always happen to me? I hopped in the car and went off to coaching. I was still coaching in the district where my former principal had hired me, except I was now coaching football, basketball, and track. Sometimes, when I had a down day teaching, my teams would bring me back up. I really needed that today.

After practice, the phone rang in the coach's office.

It was the principal.

"Lavenok, there is no easy way to say this, so I am just going to say it. The millage did not pass, and all sports are cancelled. You will not be coaching here next year."

I was numb. I took the phone and hung it up. I just sat in the chair and looked up at God and said,

"God, seriously?   Come on!   I know you only give us as much as we can handle, but I am right at that limit."

I slowly walked to my car and began my twenty-minute drive home thinking about how I was going tell my fiancé that I just lost my teaching and all my coaching jobs.

## CHAPTER 3

It was a quiet drive home, and it gave me some time to think. As I pulled the car into the carport, I slowly walked to the front door. Once I opened the door, my fiancé took one look at my face and knew something was wrong.

"What happened?" Mandy said.

"I got two calls today. I was laid off from my teaching job, and the millage did not pass, so I lost all my coaching jobs as well," I said.

"You knew going into the teaching profession that it would be like this. I think we should proceed with the wedding. It is always going to be like this, so we might as well just do it. Besides, you can do some of the stuff you always wanted to do, but couldn't because of your job or school."

Mandy was such a smart and caring woman. Her love and support only strengthened our relationship. I knew that it would be tough for us, but not this tough. We continued with our wedding plans and tried to look forward to a brighter future.

The wedding was great, and it was everything we had imagined. Instead of going on our honeymoon right away, we stayed home for a week because we wanted to enjoy the moment. We had our parents over and did all our gifts during breakfast. It was a lot of fun, and a new chapter in our lives.

We decided to go to Hawaii for our honeymoon and stop in California and stay a few days to break up the long flight. I had been saving for a few years and, we had enough money to go. I was super excited to stop in California because I wanted to stop in Santa Monica, and see the famous Gold's Gym and muscle beach. My wife was great and let me do what I wanted with those days in California. I looked up to thank God for blessing me with such a beautiful wife and just said thank you God out loud to Him. Since I did this all the time, my wife did not give it a second thought.

This is where life started to get interesting. As soon as we got back to the hotel, my phone rang. It was my principal. He informed me that I was going to be called back to teach, but it might only be for a year. I couldn't believe it. Ten minutes later, my phone rang again. It was the principal of where I coached. He said the district did another millage, and we were going to have our sports teams. Therefore, I would get all my coaching jobs back. "What luck!" I thought! Within a few minutes, I had both my teaching and coaching jobs back while we were on our honeymoon. At this moment, I knew for sure God was in my life, and was looking out for us.

The rest of the time we spent in Hawaii, and it was just beautiful, and we got home just in time to get a few things done around the house before school started.

On Saturday morning, our phone rang, and it was a principal of a rival school in my district. She said she liked what my wife had done in her long-term subbing position and wanted to interview her. My wife jumped out of bed and got ready to go.

Later that day when she walked in, she had a huge smile on her face.

"I got the job," she said.

"That is terrific! When do you start?"

"Monday," she said.

This is unbelievable I thought. I got married and went on my honeymoon with neither my wife nor I having a job.

On our honeymoon, I got both jobs back, and now my wife got a job as well. God was surely smiling down on us. This was my first lesson where I finally realized everything happens for a reason. After the school year was over, I got the dreaded pink slip again.

Mandy was right when she said I should do some stuff I always wanted to do. I figured I would try out for this show called the American Gladiators. It was a competition show with big strong guys going against average guys in tests of speed, agility, strength, and courage. I had been in shape because I always worked out and ran. So, I signed up to try out.

A buddy of mine decided to try out with me, and we drove downtown together. Once inside the building, I saw there were about 5,000 people waiting to try out as well. I said to my friend, "I think we are going to be here a while."

"I would agree," he said.

We received our number and walked to our seat. A gentleman with a black T-shirt and badge took the microphone and began to give us all directions.

"My name is David, and I will be walking you through the tryouts. There are a series of five tests, but the first test is where 90% will fail. When you are ready, we will call you down one row at a time, and you will do 60 push-ups in one minute."

"Great!" I thought. I can do that.

"The only catch is you have to do them on your finger tips," he said.

Ok, that might be a little harder than I thought, but I was able to do it. The next test was to run the 50-yard dash in five seconds or under. The only reason I tell you this is because I honestly did not think I could pass this test. I was fast, but I could not run that fast, but halfway through the run, I felt as though a very large hand was on my shoulder and gave me a push to run faster than I ever did in my life. I ran a 5 second 50 and moved on to the next round. I continued to pass all the tests and made it to the interview stage. There were only 12 other people that had made it that far before me. I felt pretty good about what I was able to accomplish.

After we were done with the interview, we left and went home. I was told they would call if we made it. Again, something strange happened. I was sitting in my room and wondering if I was going to get that call. I heard a voice inside my head telling me to call them. It was persistent, and I finally picked up the phone and made the call.

"Oh, my God," the voice on the other end of the line said. "We wanted to call you and let you know you made it, but someone spilled coffee on your phone number, and we could not read it."

"Seriously! I made it," I exclaimed.

"Yes. Be here by noon on Sunday, and we will walk you through everything."

"I will be there," I said.

The experience was great. Unfortunately, I was chosen as an alternate and only got to compete during practice. I still loved everything about it and learned a lot about myself.

Next came my basketball tryouts. I told my wife I wanted to try out for a semi-pro team and maybe work my way up to the pros. She did not laugh and said she would love to go with me. I knew it would be hard, but what the hell. I did not have a teaching job and had nothing to lose. I put all my effort into my basketball, just like I did when I was a kid.

When the day came to try out, my wife and I packed the car and drove a few hours away to where the tryouts were. It was a sight to see. There were people everywhere. When I walked into the gym, I got that feeling again and became very excited, but was also nervous. I was worried that my tryout would be quick like I experienced at the local community college.

"Ok, everyone, circle up. My name is Coach Williams. I am here to find two to three players to be on this team. Competition will be fierce, so I hope you brought your A game. You will be tested in various drills and play a lot of pickup games. We will evaluate you and let you know."

It looked like everyone was going to get a fair chance to try out. I waited and waited for him to say something else about playing in college, but it never came.

He picked up his whistle and blew it.

"Let's go ladies, what are you waiting for? Get on the baseline."

We all ran over to the baseline and began our drills. It was such a great feeling to be in the gym again playing against some great players. There were a lot of very athletic guys. I could not believe how fast they were or how high they could jump. One player even jumped right over me to put one down. That was quite embarrassing! After I played for about an hour, I started to get a little more relaxed and just relied on my instincts. I knew they would take over, and I would be able to get into that zone. I just had to get someone to pass me the ball.

Many of the players were so much stronger than I was and put on a great dunking display. I did my best to keep up and finally called for the ball. When I got it, I took a shot, and it went in. Remember, all these men here are quality players and when someone is hot, they feed them the ball. We came down the floor, and I called for the ball again. I took another shot. This time it was a three pointer. It went in. The next time down the floor, I did not have to call for the ball. They just found a way to get it to me. I ended up hitting my first six shots. Five were from the three-point line. I had earned the respect of the players and was fitting in nicely.

I continued to have a great tryout. I was hitting about 80% of my shots, averaged about ten assists, four steals, and three rebounds for the duration of the tryout.  Not bad for a guy that lasted only five minutes in a college try out.

When the final day of the try out was over, Coach Williams approached me and asked, "Hey Lavenok, where did you play your college ball?"

"I did not play college ball coach.  I had a five minute try out and that was it."

"You are good, really good, and we would like to offer you a contract to play basketball for us."

"Seriously," I said.

"Yes, seriously!  You are the best natural shooter I have ever seen and I think you can go pro if you play your cards right.  I can help you with that."

I believed him and asked him when he needed a decision. He looked at me kind of strangely, but I told him I just needed to discuss this with my wife since this decision would be affecting us both.

"Just let me know by tomorrow," he said.

"No problem.  Thanks, Coach."

This was a very tough decision for me to make. It seems like it would be an easy one since I had been wanting to play professional basketball my whole life, but it was not as easy as it should have been. My wife and I sat down to talk about it, and she asked me about my teaching job.

"What do you do about your job?" she asked.

"I don't know. Maybe take a leave of absence for a year."

"Why don't you call Tom? He may be able to give you some advice."

Again, this is where Mandy was so smart. I decided to call Tom, my old principal, and ask his advice. He told me that I would be getting my job back and probably would not be laid off again. If I decided to take a leave, I would be moved to the bottom of the seniority list and may have to wait a year.

"Mandy, what do I do? I have wanted to play basketball my whole life. I have been offered a semi-pro contract to play and the money is pretty good, but I will lose my teaching spot and may never teach again."

"Only you can decide what is best for you, but I will support you in whatever decision you make."

At this point, I know it is so cliché to say, but I felt like I was the luckiest man in the world to have that kind of support. I tried to weigh every option in my mind to make some kind of decision. I had paid for all of my own college, and it took me a little longer to get my teaching degree because of it. I liked what I did, but this was a once in a lifetime opportunity. I have always believed in listing the pros and cons, so that is exactly what I did. I guess the bottom line is that if I blew out my knee or got hurt, I would lose both my teaching job and basketball.

As tough as it was, I called Coach Williams and told him I had to decline his offer and explained why. If they would have offered me a three-year contract with about $100,000 each year, I would have taken the deal, but a one-year contract at about $75,000 would not do it. I just could not take that chance.

Just as Tom had said, I got my teaching job back and have been teaching for the last twenty years.

# CHAPTER 4

Do you ever wonder why you are here? What is your purpose? How is one's life defined? Is it by the amount of money you make? Is it the legacy you leave behind? Is it by how successful you are? Who determines what that success is?

I have often wondered what my purpose in life was. I also wondered who do I want to be, not necessarily what do I want to be. When I was younger, I wanted to be a star athlete. I had dreams of hitting that last home run or making the winning shot in a big game. All of these things were great at the time, but as I got older, my perspective on life changed. Now who I want to be is a good husband, father, co-worker, and friend. That is the legacy I want to leave behind. I would much rather have someone say, "Wow! I remember him as being a great father who always put his family first." This would be much better than, "Wow! I remember what a great athlete he was."

I also want people to remember me as being fair. That I was a person who treated everyone equally and was always there to lend a helping hand. There are times though that I just sit and think about life. Yes, I have heard several times that you are born, you live, and you die. I cannot do anything about being born or dying, but I would like to think I can do something about the living. I think about how challenging life is on a daily basis. I also try to see the simple joys in each day. A father watching his son or daughter participate in a sporting event and feeling a sense of pride. A mother lifting her child into their car seat and strapping them in. A couple holding hands while walking down the street. But, then I wonder why does it seem so many people struggle on a daily basis? Is it because we do not turn to God as often as we should? I never realized how hard life would be or how hard being a parent would be. Why does it seem that the nice guy always finishes last? How come that person gets all the breaks? Why does life always have to be so complicated? Just once, I would like to have ten minutes of peace!

After thinking about this for the longest time and calling to mind several of the books that I had read, I decided that if I really wanted my life to change, I would have to begin with myself. After all, I have to be completely honest with myself and that is not easy to do, but once I do that, hopefully, the rest will fall into place. The question is, how honest can you be with yourself? I have also learned a lot about people. I have learned that all any of us really want are basically four things. We all just want to fit in or be accepted, have people trust you, have someone believe in you, and to love and be loved. Yes, no one is perfect, and we all make mistakes, but that is how you learn. We all fail in life, but that does not necessarily mean we are failures. Everyone has the potential to be great inside of them. It is a matter of tapping that potential or learning how to release it. This leads me to what I always tell my students. I am more afraid of my kids setting their expectations too low and achieving that expectation than I am of them setting their expectations too high and failing.

This is when I began doing extensive research on the brain. I was tired of the same old routine, and I figured that the brain could be trained just like muscles could. Take geese for example. Basically, whatever living creature a gosling sees upon hatching, that is larger than itself, it thinks it is that species. This is called imprinting. What if this could be done in the human brain? What if we could alter parts of the brain that were used for specific functions? How? Where would I start?

I first began with what part of the brain I wanted to target. I narrowed my research down to six different parts of the brain. The hippocampal, the entorhinal cortex, the occipital lobes, the primary motor cortex, the premotor cortex, and the basal ganglia. Each one had a very specific function that I needed to study and use to its full potential.

The hippocampal has three regions, which are highly interconnected: the dentate gyrus, CA3, and CA1. This is the part of the brain where new neurons are developed. The dentate gyrus forms new memories that can be used by the hippocampus by taking complex neural codes from cortical areas and translating it into simper codes.

The entorhinal cortex plays a major role in memory formation. It is directly connected to the hippocampus and is the main input provider of pre-processing memorable information. Nonspatial information is transferred by the lateral part while the spatial information is transferred by the medial part. The occipital cortex is the primary visual area of the brain. Visual information such as color, orientation, and motion are transferred through the retina (via the thalamus). The occipital lobe has two different pathways, the dorsal stream and the ventral stream. The dorsal stream processes where objects are located while the ventral stream processes what objects are.

Motor movements are initiated by the primary motor cortex. Specific body parts are precisely related to different areas of the motor cortex. For instance, a person's leg movements will map to the part of the motor cortex closest to the midline. However, all body parts are not equally represented by surface area or cell density. Most of the space in the motor cortex is occupied by the arm and hand motor area. With practice/training, areas of the motor cortex can become relatively large or small.

The narrow region between the prefrontal and motor cortices is called the premotor cortex. This region is involved in preparing and executing limb movements as well as selecting appropriate movements from information it gets from other regions. Imitation as well as empathy is also learned in the premotor cortex. (This is where animal imprinting may come from.)

The basal ganglia is one of the most important pieces in the brain. It helps regulate the initiation of movements, balance, eye movements, and posture. This is extremely important in sports. There is a strong connection with the thalamus and the motor cortex. Addictive behaviors, habit formation, and reinforcement behaviors also come from the basal ganglia.

So now I knew what parts of the brain I need to manipulate or stimulate to get what I needed. Next, I need to find out the best way to do this. Also, I wanted to chemically feed the brain. I figured between the two different methods, I would be able to get the best results.

Laser light is one of the newest technologies that people are using for all kinds of different experiments. They dilate blood vessels in the area of application. When blood vessels are dilated, they carry de-oxygenated blood away and bring in freshly oxygenated blood faster. Cells will rejuvenate faster because the departing blood will also carry away bad by-products and bring in fresh cellular nutrients. I needed to make a laser light to help stimulate those six parts of my brain, but I did not know how. After doing some research, I found many people were using something called a TDCS or a transcranial direct current stimulation device. Making a TDCS from scratch seemed fairly simple, so I went to the store to get what I needed. It took a whole month of trial and error, but I figured out how to make one as well as put it in the correct spots to get direct stimulation.

Next, I needed to find out how to get the chemicals to the specific parts of my brain. This took a long time, and I researched several different types of medication. Since I knew that there were specific drugs that worked in changing the chemical balance of the brain, I focused on all the ADHD and ADD medications. There were so many to choose from, but in the end, I decided on Adderall. Not only was it a performance enhancer, and a cognitive enhancer, it increased the activity of my neurotransmitters. It lasted only four to six hours, and the side effects were minimal. I also figured that if I put it in sugar and drank it, I would get the most benefit because sugar acts as a great transport. I also used the lowest strength there was and kept adjusting until I found the right dosage.

My plan was to mix the Adderall powder in sugar water and drink it. Immediately after, I would use the TDCS to stimulate different parts of my brain. I would also watch videos or play video games to learn the moves the professional athletes were using. So basically, my brain would be open to imprinting, and since I was hitting certain parts, I would not only learn the new moves, but I would be developing new neurons. This means that I would remember all the moves I saw and pull them up when I needed them. I would be a walking computer and be able to use whatever movement I had in my so called "new library" to give me an advantage in any situation. I experimented with this for a good six months before I found the right combination. I used exactly eight ounces of cold water, 18mg of Adderall powder, and one tablespoon of sugar. I would immediately use my TDCS for a total of eighteen minutes, stimulating each of the six parts of my brain for a total of one minute three separate times. I would do ten seconds on and then ten seconds off three times until I reached a minute. After that the process would start all over again in another area of my brain. Even though the Adderall had a life span of four to six hours, I found that the best results occurred within a three-hour window. I also focused on one sport at a time. I watched every video I could find, played as many different video games that were available, and used the power of imagination to fill in the gaps. Once I saw something in the video, it was easy to imagine myself doing the same thing. How awesome would this be if it worked? I also worried that if anyone found out about this, it might endanger my family in some way or another. I think people would kill for something like this.

Every day that went by helped me to get a better understanding of what I was really trying to accomplish. I also believed I had done everything Andrew asked me to do. I continued my routine and waited for Andrew's return.

CHAPTER 5

It had been three months since I last saw Andrew, and I wondered if I imagined everything. I did what he told me to do. I got myself in the absolute best shape possible, wrote about what my life was like when I was younger, and talked a little bit about my brain research. It was very strange, because no sooner than I actually had that thought, Andrew showed up in my family room.

"Hello, Daniel," he said.

"Hey, Andrew," I replied.

"I see that you were able to do everything I asked of you. This is going to help you on your journey. Are you ready?"

"Yes, when can we get started?"

"We can get started right now. I am going to tell you what is about to happen, and we will work our way backwards. Your goal or assignment if you would like to call it that, is to get people to turn back to God."

"Turn back to God, what do you mean? Are people not praying enough? Are they worshiping someone or something else?"

"Not necessarily. God has feelings, and He wants us to turn to Him just like you want your kids to turn to you when they have a problem. He wants to have a relationship with us."

"I guess I don't understand why anyone would not turn to God if they had a problem."

"With your help, we are going to try to get people to realize that God does exist. That he is good and always will be. That he loves His children and would do anything for them. In the past, most people simply believed that God existed, and He was looking out for them. They had faith. Unfortunately, times are changing and people are changing as well."

"Ok, I get that, but how am I going to help with this? What could I possibly do to help people turn to God more?"

"You will be in God's favor, and He will give you the strength and power like no one has had for hundreds of years. People will actually be able to see what you can do and hopefully, the people that need to see to believe, will. This may come at a price. Are you willing to pay that price? Are you willing to stand up for God?"

"Yes! Just tell me what I need to do, and I will do it."

"First, let me explain a little better for you. In 1 AD, about 300,000,000 people were in the world. In 1800, about one billion people, and in 2013, about seven billion. Do you know why?"

"Sure, more and more people are getting married and having kids. Maybe they are having more than one kid. This way, the population keeps getting bigger and bigger."

"Not a bad guess, but the real reason is because people are not learning their lessons as quickly as they did before."

"Ok, now you lost me. What are you saying?"

"Heaven is a wonderful place. It is so beautiful and peaceful, that trying to explain it would not do it justice. I will give you more details later, but for now, try to imagine it as a very large school with a lot of classrooms. Each classroom is designated for a different subject. Let's say one room is for love, one is for patience, one is for compassion, etc. Each person volunteers to leave heaven and go to earth to learn that specific lesson. You cannot believe how excited the people are to get that particular experience."

"Wait, are you telling me that we have been down to earth more than once. Are you saying that we are reincarnated?"

"If that is the definition you want to use for it. Your soul is the same, but you do get a different body. You see, you find the people you are closest with in heaven, and you all agree to come down together. Sometimes it takes a while to find those people, but ultimately, you do find them. Once you do, you have lessons each day. If you pass the lesson, you move on to the next one. If you do not, you get the lesson all over again, but the next time, it will be harder. You do everything to please God and make yourself a better person. Some people are here for a day, some are here for a few years, and some are here much longer. Everything is decided and planned before you come down. You decide how long you are going to live, when you are going to come home, how you die, and so on. Nothing is left to chance."

"I always believed that we may have been here before, but I could never put my finger on certain things."

"So basically, there are more and more people in the world because it is taking them longer and longer to learn their lessons. We have tried in the past to give signs to everyone, but the few that see these signs are passed over or thought of as crazy or eccentric. Remember, Daniel, you don't have to live in the past, just learn from it."

"Can you give me an example?"

"Sure! Go to your computer right now and Google angels in clouds. You will see some pretty amazing pictures. Yes, you will see some that have been altered, but many of them are real. They are angels keeping watch over you and letting themselves be seen."

I went over to the computer and did what Andrew said. I could not believe what I had seen!

"What did you think of the pictures?"

"Wow! Those were amazing, but why don't people believe in that? I can clearly see the ones that were altered, but how can you possibly explain some of the other pictures? I can't."

"That is because you have an open mind, and you believe. It is much easier that way. Does that answer your question?"

"Yes, thank you! Ok, what is my assignment, or should I say, how am I going to go about doing my assignment?"

"You are going to be a professional athlete and play several sports."

"Andrew, people have done that before. If my memory serves me correctly, I think there were a few people that played both football and baseball."

"You are correct Daniel, but you are going to play football, basketball, baseball, and hockey, all on professional teams. You will also speak at church after communion. I will talk to you about this later."

"You are kidding me right? I am forty-five-years-old and way past my prime. I can still compete, but not at that level."

"Do you ever wonder why you never played college ball?"

"Sure, all the time. Why?"

"Every time you were on track to play, we had to push you in a different direction to make sure you were following the correct path. You and your wife were destined to be together. This is one of the reasons you did not get that scholarship. You would have moved and not ended up together."

"I know everything happens for a reason; I firmly believe that. So, you are telling me that I did not play college ball because my wife and I may not be together?"

"Yes! You have seen what your life is like now, but it would be much different if you were not together. May I ask you a question?"

"Sure!"

"Do you love your wife?"

"With all my heart!"

"Would you trade your life now for something else?"

"No!"

"Well, I think you answered your own question then. Sometimes, people do not realize that everything they ever wanted or needed was right in front of them."

"I do realize. Now, what were you saying about my assignment?"

"Daniel, you will be able to compete at that level, and you will do the most amazing things you have ever done in your life. Do you remember how you said you were more interested in who you want to be, not necessarily what you want to be?"

"Sure, I remember."

"Well, you are already the who. You have done well with that. Now it is time to be the what. You will have an opportunity to live out your wildest dreams in the sporting world, and they will be so amazing, people will have to believe. At least this is our hope. We cannot alter or play around with free will."

"This all sounds great, but I am a little skeptical. How do you propose I go about doing this? What am I going to just walk up to the coach of a professional team and say, "Hey, put me in, Coach. Watch what amazing things I can do."

"Yes, something like that."

"Are you serious?"

"Yes, I am serious. I will be right by your side the entire time, so you will have nothing to fear. Once you do this a few times, you will get more and more comfortable as time goes on. You will also get a lot of nonbelievers and a lot of people that are going to try to make your life difficult. There will be times when it will get very ugly."

"And what I am supposed to say after I do all these great things?"

"It is simple. Just say that you met an angel, he gave you special powers, and you were chosen to help people turn back to God."

"You are joking, right?"

"Yes!"

"Glad to see that you have a sense of humor. Seriously, what am I supposed to tell people?"

"Just tell people that God is with you. He is always with you and watches over you and loves you. In time, you will tell people the truth, but not just yet. We will wait and see how people react to what you say."

"Ok, Andrew, so I get this straight in my head. You are telling me that I am going to play four professional sports. I am going to not only be on those teams, but I am going to do some amazing things. I will also just one day start talking after communion at church. You want me to tell people that God is with us all, and that He loves us, and wants us to choose Him? Is that about right?"

"Yes, Daniel. You have it right! People should not be asking God for stuff. Instead, they should be asking God for guidance and help. How about we start with football, since we are in football season?"

"Sure, what do I need to do?"

"I want you to go play some pickup games and test out your new abilities. Once you get accustomed to them, we will then move on to the professional teams."

"I will call my friends up tomorrow, and we will play some football. I have not done that for a while, so it should be fun."

"Remember, Daniel, I am with you always."

CHAPTER 6

It was early Saturday morning so I called some of my buddies and asked if they would like to play some football. Just a casual pickup game at the local school down the street. I wanted to see if what Andrew had told me would really happen. How could it? I wanted to believe, but now I was the one that needed to see to believe. We picked teams and did all the regular stuff that people do before the game. We did lines, strings, or spaces to see who got the kickoff. We won, so my team went to the other end of the field and waited. What happened next was so unbelievable, I am not sure it was even real. I stood on the twenty-yard line waiting for the kickoff. I watched the ball go end over end and eventually into my arms. I then looked up and in a very brief moment, I saw the field, each player, and a path in which to run. It was like a computer screen with each specific spot mapped out. I took off running and my muscles seemed to have a mind of their own. It was like I had downloaded a computer program to my muscles, and they just followed. I spun, turned, cut in different directions, and as unbelievable as it sounds, was not touched until the high fives for scoring a touchdown. I was really excited after this, but was it luck or could I do this again? The game went well, and I did things I was not able to do since I was a kid, and some of them I was never able to do. I needed to do another test with different people, so I figured I needed to find another game.

I spent some time on Sunday driving to local high schools trying to find a game I could join. I found one about ten minutes away from my house. There was a group of about nineteen or twenty guys playing. I got out of my car, and they stopped the game and kind of looked at me strangely. I asked the guys if I could join the game. I told them I was doing an experiment for school and just wanted to get out and play. It did not matter what team I was on or what position I played.

"Sure, no problem, said one of the boys. My name is Brenden."

"My name is Daniel. Nice to meet all of you." I said.

After that we played for a while. It was just like I was in a video game. No matter what position I was in, I could see where I was supposed to be and my muscles followed. I asked if I could take the kickoff because I wanted to see what would happen. To my delight, I watched the ball go end over end and eventually into my arms. I then looked up and in a very brief moment, I saw the field, each player, and a path in which to run. I ran and scored a touchdown untouched. I did this in two separate games, with different people in each game. It had to be real! Andrew was right; the more I did, the more confident I became. I went home and sat down and called for Andrew.

"Andrew, are you there?"

"I am here, Daniel."

"So, did you see? Of course you saw, sorry, that was a dumb question."

"No, that was not a dumb question, and yes, I did see. Do you think you are ready now to try your skills at a professional level?"

"Yes, I am ready. I will go tomorrow to the practice facility and somehow convince them to let me try out."

"Remember, Daniel, we are with you. I want you to feel the strength and love of God. When you do, you will do well."

It was Monday morning, and we had no school. I needed to keep my promise, so I said goodbye to my wife and took off for the practice facility. I knew I had her one hundred percent support. She knew everything and just gave me this look and said good luck.

The drive out to the facility gave me a chance to think and reflect on some of the stuff that had happened as well as some of my conversations with Andrew. I guess I could not believe what he was saying about people turning away from God. I get it, but don't understand it. I sometimes get as unhappy as the next guy and often feel like a failure to my family. I know that being a teacher is a great job, and I feel like I have helped many kids, but it is hard to always fight for what I believe to be right and just. I don't blame God for any of this. On the contrary, I embrace Him more, for I feel that He is the one that put me on this path, and I am following what He wants me to do with my life.

Before I knew it, I had reached the parking lot. "Ok, how I am going to do this. They are going to think I am crazy. Who cares? I have angels on my side," I thought. I opened the car door and began walking towards the practice facility. I was approached by a security guard. His name badge said Isaac, and he asked me what I was doing there. I told him I needed to speak to the coach for just five minutes. The answer was no.

"Coach is too busy," he said.

"Please, I only need five minutes. Ah, come on, Isaac, I promise I will not embarrass you. I will also give you credit when this works out."

"When what works out?" he asked.

"I am going to play football for this team, and when I do, I will make sure I let everyone know that it was you that helped. After all, the best thing you can give someone is a chance!"

"Are you crazy?" he asked.

"You bet! Crazy in a good way. Come on, aren't you the least bit curious?"

"You have two minutes to leave, or I am calling the police."

"Please, I was sent here by an angel. I just need five minutes. Search your heart, and I know you will believe in me."

Andrew must have helped in some way because Isaac seemed to change his mind.

"Ok, you have my attention. What is five minutes going to hurt? Wait here, please."

After about ten minutes, he came back with one of the assistant coaches.

"How can I help you?" he asked.

"My name is Daniel, and I would like to try out for your team."

He literally looked at me with the strangest look and just turned around and started walking away.

"Excuse me!"

He stopped and looked back.

"Listen, I know how this sounds, but if you give me just five minutes to prove myself, I promise, I will not make a fool of you."

"Listen, Daniel. We don't hold try outs, and we certainly would not take someone as old as you. I appreciate whatever joke or dare you are doing, but we are done here. Have a great day!"

With this he started to walk away again. I was stunned. I thought this would have gone better.

"Andrew, a little help here please," I said.

With that, instantly, I knew what to say.

"Hey Coach! Do you remember your senior year in high school? The quarterback was not playing well and you thought for sure you would get your shot. Unfortunately, your coach did not give it to you until the quarterback got hurt. It was halfway through the season, and you thought you should have been given a shot earlier."

"How do you know that? Not even my wife knows that story."

"As I told Isaac, an angel sent me. I will make a deal with you. Give me one play, just one play, and if I don't score a touchdown on that one play, I will leave and never come back. Seriously, what do you have to lose? Nothing! If I don't score, you can chalk it off as giving an old guy a chance to fulfill a dream. If I do score, you will be a genius. Come on, what do you say? You pick the play, and I will score. One of the most important things you can give someone is a chance."

"Ok, I will give you one play. I am not sure why I am doing this, but what the hell! You say any play?"

"Any play and I will score."

"Come with me. We will do a kickoff. I figure that is the hardest and longest. I need you to sign some forms in case you get hurt. We don't want to be responsible for anything."

"Just lead the way."

With that I followed him to an office to sign the paper work. After that, I went into the locker room, where they gave me some equipment. It was weird to be in a locker room again. I had not put on a full football uniform since I was in junior high school. Putting those pads on and taking my shoes out of my bag brought back so many memories. It was very healing. As I walked out of the locker room and through the tunnel, it was one of the best feelings I had ever experienced. I jogged over to the middle of the field where the coach was talking to the head coach. I am not real sure what the conversation was, but the head coach just walked away with his arms in the air.

Coach Matthew called the special teams unit over and explained what was going to happen. He told the kickoff team that I guaranteed I would score on one play. This did not sit too well with the players. They looked like they wanted to kill me. He asked the return team to give it their best shot and block for me. "Just one play," he said to them.

"One play and we can get back to our practice."

At this point my heart was racing. I was nervous as hell. "What have I just gotten myself into," I thought? I began to doubt myself and started to think about leaving. At this point, I saw Andrew standing right in front of the football. He just smiled and said.

"I am with you, Daniel. You can do this."

With that I ran back and stood on the twenty-yard line waiting for the kickoff. I watched the ball go end over end and eventually into my arms. I then looked up and in a very brief moment, I saw the field, each player, and a path in which to run. It was exactly the same as it was in the pick-up games I had played. I took off running and just let my body do the work. It was unbelievable. I went untouched and scored on an eighty-yard run. All the players on the kickoff team were stunned.

"Hey, Coach, that was just luck. Can we run it again?" one of the players said.

"Run it again," he screamed.

For the next six kickoffs, I did the exact same thing. I scored a touchdown! By this time, I think I had a few players on the team that started to believe. I did not want any of this day to end. It was one of the greatest feelings in the world, and I owed it all to Andrew. Once I had scored on the last play, the head coach came over and asked how I did what I did. I told him that I had God on my side, and I would love to do the same thing for him in a game.

"Did an angel really send you? Can you do the same thing in our game next Sunday?" he asked.

"Yes, sir and Yes, sir," I replied.

With that, he sent me to sign a ten-day contract to be part of the team and told me to show up a few hours before the game.

When I got home I told my wife what had happened. She could not believe it.   She had been through so much with my sporting events.   She was always there to support and encourage me.   Finally, something good was going to happen, but Andrew said it might get difficult. Hopefully not, but whatever awaited us, we would get through it!

CHAPTER 7

"Are you sure you will be ok? Are you sure Andrew will be there?"

"Yes, he will be there. Please don't worry. I will be fine. Besides, this is exciting. Please let my parents know and bring the kids. I will get some tickets and have them at the ticket counter so you can all sit together."

I showed up early and walked the field. I had never been on the football field of a professional stadium before. It was a great feeling. I looked around and imagined what it would be like to see so many people in the stands. I became more excited as time went on. Around this time, some of the other players began to show up. Even though I may have helped them, they were not at all friendly. A few of them were great, but the vast majority did not give me the time of day.

As we started to get dressed, I just sat on the chair next to my locker. I could not believe what was happening to me. I kept reminding myself that this was real. It was not a dream. In a few minutes, I would be on the field with professional athletes who were looking to rip my head off. I don't care who you are, or who is with you. At this point, I was really nervous, but excited at the same time. Running out of that tunnel was one of the greatest experiences I have had in a very long time. I took my time running on the field and was one of the last ones to approach the sideline. As I went to the huddle, the coach said he was sending out the captains to do the coin toss. We watched and saw the ref signal that we would receive the kickoff. At this point, my nerves were getting to me a little. Yes, everything that Andrew said would happen did. I was able to score in the pick-up games, as well as at the practice facility, but nothing prepared me for this. The crowd was absolutely amazing. I cannot even begin to describe the atmosphere. Excitement, nerves, energy, noise, it was just incredible.

"Ok, Lavenok, let's see if you can duplicate what you did the other day," he said.

"I will give it my best shot Coach."

With that answer, I looked around for Andrew. He was standing right in front of the football, just like he did before. I had a smile on my face when I ran onto the field.

"Hey, Lavenok, what the hell you smilin' about?"

"Oh nothing, I answered. Just smiling because I know God is on my side, and I am going to score a touchdown."

"Well, you're gonna need all the help you can get!"

To my delight, I watched the ball go end over end and eventually into my arms. I then looked up and in a very brief moment, I saw the field, each player, and a path in which to run. It was identical to what I had experienced before. I ran and scored a touchdown untouched. It was simply awesome!

I could hear the crowd going wild. I saw Coach Matthew look over to the assistant coach and just shake his head. I watched the replay on the big screen and heard one announcer say, "Who is this guy?" to the other announcer.

We had three kick returns and two punt returns that day. I scored on all five plays. The coach was dumfounded at the press conference.

"Hey, Coach, where did you get this Lavenok from? What college did he play for? Was he on the practice squad?"

"Actually, it is kind of a funny story. He was at our practice facility and approached Isaac, one of our security guards. He then told my assistant coach that some nut job wanted to try out for the team. He said he could score on any play because God was on his side."

"And, you actually let him try?"

"Well, our assistant was not real sure what to do. However, Lavenok convinced him to give him just five minutes. If he did nothing, what did we really lose? We all have five minutes. If he did score, the credit would go to both our security guard and assistant coach. He scored six times in a row. He said something that made us all think. He said that the greatest thing we can give someone is a chance. I guess he was right!"

"Are you going to play him again next week?"

"I think so," the coach said.

"Can we talk to him?" a reporter asked.

"Sure," Coach Matthew said.

"Hey, Lavenok, how did you do that? Where did you play before? Did you play any college ball?"

"Thank you for asking some great questions. Before I continue, I need to thank Isaac and assistant Coach Thaddeus. They gave me this chance.

I looked over to both of them and nodded my head. Both men stood up a little straighter and simply smiled.

"This is my first press conference. To answer some of your questions, I did not play anywhere. I did not play in college, and I have God on my side."

"God on your side, what do you mean by that?"

I saw Andrew in the back of the room shake his head. Then he put a thought in my head. "People may not be ready to hear the truth, but go ahead and try."

"I mean God is on my side. I am blessed to have Him with me."

"Yeah, I get it. All the athletes thank God and say He is on their side."

Andrew looked at me and again put another thought in my head. "They are not ready yet, so just leave it at that."

"Thank you very much for coming, and I hope I get a chance to talk to you all again. Have a great day!"

With that I walked out and went into the locker room to change. I could not wait to see my family and see how they felt. I also wanted to talk to Andrew. After I finished changing I had a chance to talk to my wife.

"Wow! That was simply amazing! How are you feeling right now?"

"I know, right. I can't believe it myself. I cannot even describe to you how I am feeling. It is like nothing I have ever felt before."

"That is great! What is next?"

"I have to talk to Andrew and see what my next step is. Let's go get something to eat."

After dinner we went home, and I could hardly wait to talk to Andrew. I went into the den and called for him.

"Hello, Daniel!"

"Hey, Andrew. How did I do?"

"You did great, but you know that was your one and only game, right?"

"No, I did not know that. Why? Why do I only get one game?"

"Our goal is to get people to turn back to God. If you were to play more than one game, people would be talking about what you did instead of wondering how you did it. You will move on to basketball now. We will do exactly what you did for football."

"But, Andrew, if I do that for basketball, won't people just say I got lucky? Won't they just think that I might have been in a zone or on steroids or something?"

"Daniel, we cannot influence free will. If that is what people want to believe, that is what they are going to believe. You cannot change how they think. Your job is to make them think."

"Ok, I guess I understand. I have learned to trust God and not ask why. Although that is very hard to do sometimes? Hey, Andrew, may I ask you a question?"

"Sure! What would you like to know?"

"What is heaven really like?"

"That is a tough question to answer. It is hard to picture something so beautiful without ever seeing it. The colors are so amazing. When you go to heaven, you leave your body and go back to a very simple yet unbelievable form. You can see everyone and everything on earth, but they cannot see you. You see and feel things at an extremely magnified level. It is the most peaceful place you can ever imagine, and it is filled with love. It is so hard to put into words what it is like. I am sorry, Daniel! That probably did not answer your question."

"It helps. I kind of had a picture in my mind, and your answer just helps to clarify it. I was just wondering. May I ask you one more question?"

"Sure!"

"When you die, do you remember your life on earth?"

"Another good question. The simple answer, yes! You remember all your lives and everyone you have ever met. You take the lessons you have learned and all your feelings. Love, compassion, sympathy, etc. Love is the strongest and the minute you are welcomed home, it is like your soul is plugged into heaven, and it is being fed love. This is one of the reasons why angels glow. I guess the best advice I could give you is love and be loved, have patience with people, and build relationships. Love and relationships are two very important things you take with you. In fact, when you are getting ready to cross over, most people want the people they have been closest to around them. I cannot ever remember anyone asking for any materialistic things to comfort them at the very end."

"I kind of figured that, but it is always nice to get confirmation."

"Remember, Daniel, your time here is limited. It seems like a very long time to you because you are living it day by day, but in reality, it goes by very quickly. As hard as it may get sometimes, God is always with you."

"Thank you, Andrew. Even though I know that, it is nice to hear it from an angel."

"Are you ready to move on to basketball?"

"Yes, but how do I tell Coach Matthew that I will not be returning?"

"You just call him up and tell him thank you for giving you a chance. Deep down he will know it is the right decision."

With that, Andrew said goodbye and I picked up the phone to call Coach Matthew. I told him how much I appreciated the chance, but I needed to continue on with my assignment. He wished me the best and said he would always have a spot on the team for me if I ever changed my mind.

CHAPTER 8

I loved football and was pretty good at it, but basketball was my true love. I played all the time and honestly thought I would be a professional basketball player some day. I knew that this task would be even more difficult than football, but I was ready for the challenge. I woke up early Saturday morning reflecting on the crazy few weeks that I had just gone through. I felt I needed to talk to Andrew to get more direction. Sure enough, there he was!

"Hi, Andrew."

"Hi, Daniel. How are you feeling today?"

"Ok, I guess. I am a little nervous about this basketball thing. I am not sure I can just walk up to the coach and ask to be put on the team. How am I going to do this?"

"You were always a good basketball player. You were good enough to go pro. You just never did. You will get all the ability back and you will shoot 90% from the floor and 100% from the free throw line. That should get their attention."

"Ok, sounds good. Hey Andrew, I am only six feet tall, but I can jump, and I dunked a volleyball once. Will I be able to dunk now?"

"Unfortunately, no. You will have your same abilities, but they will be amplified."

"Ah mannnn! I thought I would be able to dunk. I guess we can't have all our dreams."

"I would like you to do the same thing you did in football. I want you to find some pick-up games and just go play. Get your feel for the game back, and then I will check back with you. This time, you will need to add more in your press conference since this will be your second professional sport. Hopefully, you will get people thinking."

"Ok, sounds good! I will look for some games later on today and tomorrow and talk to you on Monday."

After talking to my wife and letting her know my next assignment, I went off to find some basketball games. While I was driving in the car, I was wondering what it would be like to sit down and have a conversation with Jesus. I figured I would ask Andrew the next time I talked to him about this. I was curious what his answer would be.

After driving for a little while, I ended up at the local park. People were always playing games on these courts, and I figured I would just wait my turn and get into a game. I found a parking spot and turned off the car. I reached into the back seat and grabbed my bag and headed to the court. While I was putting on my basketball shoes, I could not help but get excited about playing again. How was this going to work? How good was I really going to be? After about fifteen minutes of waiting, it was my turn to head into the game. We made our introductions, and off I went. After playing for about five minutes I got my playing legs back. I finally got an open look at the basket and took my shot. It went in! "Ok," I thought, I can normally do that. As the game proceeded, I began to get more and more confidence. I was doing cross overs, passes behind my back, no look passes, and I could not miss. I decided to really test my abilities and do an impossible shot. I would drive the baseline, wait to be pushed out of bounds, and take a shot from behind the backboard.

I could not believe that the ball went in. I played for a few hours and made every single shot I took. It was awesome, but weird at the same time. The guys on the other team started thinking they were being punked or were on some kind of reality TV show. After a while, many of them just walked off the court and waited for me to leave.

I figured I had proved to myself I was ready, but wanted one more test. After all, I did at least two pick-up games for football, and Andrew said I should do basketball the same way. I thanked the guys for playing with me and walked to the car to get ready for my drive home.

Later that night, I decided to go to a gym that a former professional basketball player owns and jump into some games there. I knew the talent would be just as good or better as on the outdoor courts. I walked in, sat down, and began to put on my basketball shoes. I waited my turn and jumped into a game. It was a little faster paced than yesterday, but I was able to keep up. I was not tired at all and was able to do similar things I did the day before. I was doing cross overs, passes behind my back, no look passes, and I could not miss. I continued for about two hours and just enjoyed playing. After a while, I had many of the guys asking me where I played my college ball or how was I able to make all my shots. I told them I had God on my side and most of them thought I was crazy, but a few did believe me. Once I finished, I started to head to my car for my drive home. Little did I know that one of the NBA professional scouts were there. He saw me play and was asking people questions about me.

After I got home, I talked to Mandy for a little while. She said the kids were doing homework so we had a little time to catch up on the day. I asked her if she was ok with everything I was doing.

"So far," she said.

"What if people begin to really think I am crazy? What if I lose my job?"

"Hopefully, none of that will happen, but if this is God's will, it is God's will. We will do whatever is necessary."

"I am so lucky to have you in my life and even luckier to have your support."

"That is what a marriage is."

We talked for a little while longer, and then I told her I needed to get ready for my impromptu tryout tomorrow. After I woke up on Sunday, I told Mandy goodbye and began my drive to the basketball arena. It would give me some time to think how I would approach this situation. I knew it would not be easy, but maybe the coach had seen me play football and this might be easier to get on the team. As I approached my parking spot, I took a deep breath and got out of the car. I grabbed my bag from the back seat and began to walk to the door. The practice facility was behind the main building, so I headed for the front door. As soon as I went to open the door, I was approached by a gentleman named Jacob. He knew why I was there and explained to me that he saw me play the day before. He also saw me on TV and told the coach that they might be getting a visit from me.

"Are you Lavenok?"

"Yes sir," I answered.

"Well, I saw you play, and we are looking forward to seeing what you can do. You ready?"

"You bet!"

"The locker room is over there. Change and meet me out here in ten minutes please."

"Will do!"

As I walked into the locker room, I could feel my heart starting to pound a little harder. I could not believe this was happening. I had waited all my life for this moment and hoped I would not let myself down. I shut the locker and headed for the court. Once I was there, I looked around for Andrew. He was standing by the storage room and just gave me a smile.

"Lavenok, this is Coach Mark."

"Hi, Coach!"

"Can you do what you did the other day today?"

"I think so! I will definitely give it my best shot."

"Great! Get out there for Henderson, and let's see what you can do."

The game went just like the other two days I had played. I got into a major zone and did not miss one shot. I ran the floor well, stole a few passes, had a few assists, and even a few rebounds. It was absolutely unbelievable. I was even shocked. After playing for about fifteen minutes, coach told us to stop and called me over.

"Lavenok, I am going to sign you to a five-day contract. You look like you can add a spark to this team, and you look very hungry."

"Thank you, Coach! I guess when you have had this dream for such a long time, you appreciate every moment you get. I am hungry. I want to step out on that floor for just one game and prove that I can play. That is all I need."

"Well, we certainly hope it is for more than one game. Be here a few hours early for our shoot around, and I will see you in two days."

I thanked the coach and walked back to the locker room. As I was changing, I was running the events of the day through my mind. I wanted to talk to Andrew. I thought I was having more fun and was worried I was not doing what I had been asked to do. I grabbed my stuff and headed to the car for my drive home.

CHAPTER 9

After I got home, Mandy asked how the try out went. I told her, and she was excited, but also nervous at the same time. I asked her why she was nervous, and she told me she was worried about the press conference.

"What are you going to say when people recognize you? What are you going to tell them?"

"I think I am going to tell them the truth. I know people will probably think I am crazy, but do you really think Andrew would have me do all this and then have bad stuff happen to us?"

"I don't think so, but I am still concerned about what people are going to say and how they are going to react. This is something people hear every day, but it is different when someone is standing in front of a bunch of people and actually saying it."

As usual, Mandy was right. I was a little concerned as well, but I had total confidence in Andrew. At that moment, I told Mandy I was going to talk to him to help ease both of our minds. Once I was in the den, Andrew appeared and asked me how I was doing.

"I am fine, Andrew. I know you just heard our conversation, so what do I say to help ease her mind?"

"Daniel, do you have your poem book?"

"What?" I asked.

"Your poem book! Do you still have it somewhere that you can just go get it?"

"Yes, why?"

"Please just go get it. I want to show you something."

"Ok, I will be right back."

I ran up to our bedroom and took my poem book out of my nightstand. I used to write poems to help me get through some of the rough times in my life. I don't really like to talk about them, so putting it down on paper was the next best thing for me.

"Can you open it up to your last poem please?"

"Sure!"

"What is the name of the last poem?"

"It is called Best Friend."

"Can you read it for me please?"

"Andrew, what does this have to do with anything?"

"Please, Daniel, just read it. You will understand very shortly."

With that I began to read the last poem.

"I watched my best friend die today,

it was something I will never forget.

I was thinking of all the great times we had,

especially the first time that we met.


The last moments of his life were hard for him,

and I know it took tremendous will.

For at the exact moment he passed away,

it felt as through time stood still.


I didn't know what to do or say,

my best friend was gone for now.

I wanted to trade places to help my friend,

but couldn't figure out how.

So I sat down to talk to God,

To see what I could do.

He told me to lie down in my bed,

And he would take me too.


When I got to heaven and saw these things,

I'd never seen before.

An angel came and signaled me,

And we went through the final door.


I saw my friend standing by a pond,

Looking peaceful as could be.

And then he turned to look ahead,

and see if it was me.


I told him that I owed him one,

and I would stay for good.

I told him that I would now go,

and stand where he once stood.

He looked at me with a smile,

and replied, "That's nice of you."

But would not let me do the things,

that I had wanted to.


He told me that it wasn't time,

for my life to come to an end.

And then he sent me back to live,

my life with no best friend."


"Do you remember writing this poem, Daniel?"

"Yes, why?"

"Because it was not a dream, it really happened."

"Which part?"

"All of it. Please look at this specific part of the poem.

When I got to heaven and saw these things,

I'd never seen before.

An angel came and signaled me,

And we went through the final door.

"When you got to heaven, that angel was me. I was the one you saw. Search your heart. You know this to be true."

I could not believe my ears. I was in total shock. It was one of those moments when you are like holy crap! I did have a best friend that died, but I thought I dreamed all the rest.

"You always try to put everyone else before yourself, but in this particular situation, you really went above and beyond. We knew at this moment you might be one of the many around the world we would be calling on to help. It was just a matter of time."

"Wow! I cannot believe that was you. I guess I always knew, but could never put it all together. Thank you for believing in me!"

"No, thank you, Daniel! We were with you then; we are with you now, and we will be with you in the future. Please, tell Mandy not to worry!"

## CHAPTER 10

After that discussion with Andrew, I did not know if I was more excited to play in the game or know that I was helping out. I wanted to really enjoy this moment because I knew it would never happen again. Sometimes, the road to your destination is just as exciting as the final outcome. I knew the game would be great, but the anticipation of playing and everything leading up to it was simply awesome. I tried to take in every moment, from getting up and getting ready, going to work, and driving to the arena after dinner.

Mandy, the kids, and my family were going to meet me later before the game. It was exciting for them as well. I arrived at the arena after a twenty-minute drive. I got a chance to park in the player's parking lot. It was great! I grabbed my backpack and began my walk to the back door. Once inside, I could sense the excitement I was getting from being able to fulfill one of my life long dreams. The guys in the locker room were ok towards me. They obviously saw me at practice, but were not very welcoming. I don't blame them. I don't think I would like some older guy coming in and taking time away from me.

A few minutes later, Coach Mark came into the locker room and told us this was a pretty big game and just go out and play.

"You ready for this, Lavenok?" he asked.

"Yes, sir! I will give you my best."

Once we left the locker room, we went down a long hall. I could hear the crowd. As we got closer, I could feel my heart racing. I was getting very nervous. Yes, I know what Andrew said, and I openly apologized to him, but I was still nervous. I could see the court now. We all began to jog and then get into our layup lines. I was doing layups with a professional basketball team, on a professional court, in a professional game. I had made it. Now, the next thing I had to do was get into the game. Finally, I needed to do what I was asked to do.

The ref blew the whistle, and we began to play. We were doing ok, but had a hard time moving the ball around. It was great to just sit on the end of the bench and take everything in. I looked around for Mandy and my family, and finally spotted them about fifteen rows up. She was smiling at me and then just gave me that look. I knew exactly what it meant, and I was ready to go into the game. I also looked around for Andrew. He was right under the visiting basket. He just kind of gave me a smile, and I knew I was going to do something great!

"Lavenok, get your butt in for Fisher."

I quickly jumped off the bench and removed my warm-ups and ran to the scorer's table.

"Number 13 checking in," I said.

"Next ball stop, be ready," he said.

I waited patiently. It seemed like forever, but a few minutes later, there was a stop, and I entered the game. Only my family clapped because they were the only ones who knew who I was. After a few minutes, I began to relax and let my instincts take over. It was just like in the practices. After about six minutes of playing, I got the ball with an open look. I took my shot, and it went in. We went down, and I stole the ball. We had a fast break, and I made a great behind the back pass, and Johnson jammed it home.

"Nice pass man!"

"Awesome dunk!"

We continued to play for another few minutes, and I was really starting to feel comfortable. The second quarter was my quarter. I scored twenty points. I kept making shot after shot. They would find a way to get me the ball and set some great screens and picks. I made every shot I took. Finally, one of their players was so angry, he gave me a hard foul. When I got up, I wiped the blood away from my nose and lip. It instantly brought me back to high school when I had a similar thing happen. Except this time, I did not have to worry about a parent calling me out.

"Lavenok, you ok? "Coach asked.

"Yeah, fine coach."

"Make these two, and we will get you fixed up at halftime."

"No problem Coach!"

After I made both free throws, we headed into the locker room with a ten-point lead. We all sat down and waited for Coach Mark to give his speech.

"You guys are playing great. Just keep getting back on defense, controlling the boards, and looking for one another. The fast break is working so keep pushing the ball."

After half, we ran back out to the court to do our warm ups. I did not want this night to end. I tried to remind myself that I was actually in the game. It was really happening. I continued my hot streak and scored another ten points in the third quarter and did not miss a shot.

Heading into the fourth quarter, Coach Mark asked me,

"Lavenok, you got anything left?"

"You bet coach. The only way I am coming out of this game is on a stretcher."

The fourth quarter was just like the third quarter. I scored another fifteen points and the game came down to the last minute. It was tied when the coach called a time out.

"Get the ball to Lavenok. He will take the last shot."

We came out of the time out and walked back on the court. I figured the other team knew I was going to get the ball. We set up our play and they worked the ball to me with about twenty seconds left. I got a high screen, dribbled to my right and went up for the shot. While in the air, I saw Morris break for the basket. His guy left him alone to double team me, so I passed to him. He had an easy layup and the game was over. We had won! We all piled on each other and celebrated a great win. When the game was over, I went to the locker room to change and head to the press conference. I knew this was going to be tough, but I was ready.

"Hey, Lavenok, you scored 45 points in your first game. How do you explain that?"

"Luck I guess!"

"Seriously, last week you played professional football and scored five times. What is your secret?"

I had to think about this for a minute. I wanted to make sure I said what I was supposed to say. I looked around for Andrew. He was at the back of the room and just nodded his head. I figured I would give the real answer this time.

"To be honest, I am doing God's work. I was approached by an angel. His name is Andrew, and he told me that I would help turn people back to God. We are using sports to do that."

I could hear the comments begin to start. People were laughing and looking around to see if they were on some kind of reality show. After a few minutes, they began to realize I was not joking.

"I ask you a serious question, and you come back with some crazy story. I think you owe us more than that. You scored five touchdowns, last week and 45 points this week. Not to mention you did it in two professional sports. That is not a coincidence. We want to know what is going on. Are you on some experimental drug? What are you doing that is different than anyone else?"

"As I told you before, an angel approached me and told me we needed to get more people to turn back to God, and they were going to use me with sports as a way to do this. It is the truth. Whether or not you believe me is totally up to you."

"You're serious!"

"Yes, I am serious, and I am going to play professional baseball and hockey as well. God wants people to know that He wants us to turn to Him in times of need. Not to ask for stuff, but rather lean on Him. He also wants us to learn patience."

Man, this guy was a total jerk. What was his problem? He did not let anyone else ask any questions. I tried to get other people involved in the press conference, but he was the one that kept pushing.

"Ok, Lavenok, you can't say that God is helping you because He is here for everyone. Why can't you just tell us the truth? What makes you so special? Are you saying you are better than everyone?"

"I am telling you the truth and no, I am no different than anyone else. No better than anyone else. I was approached by an angel and told what was going to happen. I am simply trying to give an answer to your question."

I looked around to see if there were any more questions, but this guy would not stop.

"May I ask your name," I said to the gentleman.

"Sure! My name is Joshua."

"Joshua, I cannot help whether or not you believe me, but that is the truth. I don't want to hold up this press conference any longer. Maybe you and I can talk after."

"Sure!"

With that, the press conference was over, and I began to head to my car. As soon as I walked out the door, I saw Joshua walking toward me.

"Ok, Lavenok, can I have the truth now? What are you doing that is so different than anyone else? I promise it will stay with just me."

"As I told you at the press conference, I was approached by an angel and I am trying to get people to turn back to God. It is as simple as that."

"Man, you are full of crap. I am going to find out what is going on here. Both you and I know that you are hiding something, and it may take some time, but I will get to the bottom of this."

"Feel free, Joshua. Let me know if you need anything else because you will find nothing since there is nothing to find. I told you the truth. Why is it so hard to believe something when God is involved? This is exactly what I am trying to change."

With that I got into my car and drove off to meet my wife and kids in the parking lot.

## CHAPTER 11

It was a quiet drive home. I kept thinking about what just happened. Last week I was a professional football player. I scored five times, and it was simply awesome. This week I was a professional basketball player. I did not just play, but scored 45 points in one game. I have no words to describe what was happening to me. I could not wait to get home and speak to Andrew. I wanted to see if I was making a difference.

Once I got home, my wife and kids congratulated me and told me how proud of me they were. It was a very special moment, a moment that is burned into my memory and will never be forgotten. After we were all done, I went into the den to talk to Andrew.

He was already there waiting for me.

"Congratulations, Daniel. You have done well with your assignment so far, and we are proud of you. There are some that are starting to believe, but we still have many others that do not."

"What else can I do Andrew?"

"Just keep doing what you are doing and hopefully, people will wake up."

"Andrew, can I ask you a question?"

"Sure!"

"How does God look at people? Ok, let me try to clarify. I know there are different religions, and there are even people that do not believe in God. How does He look at that? What does He think?"

"Wow, that is a very tough question, and the answer may surprise you. There is no religion better than another. In heaven, there is only one religion. When you are down here on earth, you need several religions because people are at different levels. This is not saying different religions are at different levels. It is saying that people are at different spiritual levels, and their religion is geared to their level. God is disappointed because people do not believe in Him. Do you remember when you said you have learned a lot about people? All any of us really want are basically four things. We all just want to fit in or be accepted, have people trust you, have someone believe in you, and to love and be loved."

"Yes, I remember that."

"Well, God feels the same way."

"I guess I never really looked at it that way before."

"Let me try to give you a little more insight.   God feels one purpose of human life is to serve and show compassion toward one another.  He also believes you should have a strong desire to help others.  Some people realize this, and it shows by the type of profession they go into.  You once said you were more interested in who you became instead of what.  Well sometimes, God is more impressed with why you do something rather than what you do."

"Can you give me an example?"

"I will try.  Your wife is sick, and you go to the store to get her some medicine.  What did you do?"

"I went to the store to get medicine."

"Right, but why did you do it?"

"Because my wife needed it."

"This is an example of Him being more impressed with the why and not the what. I know it is a little quirky, but you understand my point don't you?"

"Yes, I do!"

"People are always thinking they are the ones in control. God gives them what they need when they need it. Understand, Daniel, not every question will have an answer, and you will go through life with things that you just don't understand. That is ok because of faith. If you believe that everything happens for a reason, then you will be able to move on. Do God's will and ask Him to guide you. Don't do your own will, and ask God to help you. We talked about how you decide everything about this life before you come down. What most people fail to realize is they just don't remember what they agreed to do, but it is necessary for their growth. It takes some people a long time to trust God and begin to do His work. They fight with themselves each and every day because they are doing what they think is best for themselves instead of doing what is best for God. When people really learn to go within, and give themselves over to trusting God, their lives will be that much more satisfying. Daniel, what do you think is more important, having personal power or positional power?"

"I guess that depends on your situation. I would say that the president has a lot of positional power and his decisions affect millions."

"You are correct! So, you think positional power is more important?"

"I am not sure. I once heard someone say is it harder to conquer a city than your mind. So, if that statement is true, I would have to say personal power?"

"Sometimes, we answer our own questions."

"I think I understand. Are you just trying to tell me to simply trust God and try to live my life and accept whatever happens?"

"Yes and no! Remember, your decisions will have a profound effect on your life, so choose wisely. Your life is mapped out, but we cannot control free will. People need to do what they need to do because they want to do it."

"Well, that is certainly a mouthful."

"Earlier, we talked about religion and how there are different levels because people are at different levels. Once we learn not to judge each other, we will live a much richer life."

"Judge each other how?"

"You have heard that all people are created equally. Well, there is no one group of people or single individual that is better than another. Each person that is here, is here for a purpose. However, we tend to classify people by how they look, what they do, how much money they make, etc. This is simply wrong, and if people knew their entire plan, they would realize that those people who come into their life do so for a reason, to help their growth. God does not judge, people judge."

"How do we get people to change this?"

"It is hard to change people. You told everyone the truth. You said you saw an angel, and many did not believe you. In fact, they think you are hiding something. If you told them you saw a UFO, would they believe that more? We find it interesting that when it comes to God, it is so much harder to believe."

"Well, that is sad."

"This is one of the reasons we choose you to help us. You are not the only one. Each person that is helping is doing so in a different way."

"Andrew, I am kind of worried. I know I probably should not ask this question, but I am going to anyway. I am sorry! Why is God doing this?"

"Every few hundred years, people lose their way, and they just need a little help finding their way back. We have done this for thousands of years, but it is getting harder and harder each time because people are changing so quickly."

"Can you give me an example of someone who did this before?"

"Sure, but I cannot give you a name. It is against the rules."

"Ok, that is fine."

"In early 1800 there were so many people that lost their way, it was much harder to get them back on track. It is so much harder when the people who lose their way are in positions of power. In this case, people saw their country, their world, moving in a different direction. They wanted all people to see everything in the way they did. This is when the Civil War broke out. One of the people we approached was able to help change the war and eventually unite each state."

"I think I know who you are talking about. You have to forgive me for saying this, but that is kind of a bizarre story. If it is the person I think it is, all I can say is wow!"

"I am sure you are probably correct in the person that you are thinking, but I assure you, it did happen. There were several people involved, but this person had the most impact."

"So you are saying that this has happened throughout time?"

"Yes, people will surprise you when given the proper chance. Let me give you a quote by someone who figured out life at a very early age. He was so right on, it is scary. He said "The two most important days in your life are the day you are born and the day you figure out why." This was said by Mark Twain, and it is the absolute truth."

"That is a pretty interesting quote."

"Yes, it is!"

"Are there any other ways that God communicates with us?"

"Yes, He uses your dreams."

"I always thought there was something with our dreams. How is it I can fly in my dreams, walk through walls, imagine I am somewhere and instantly I am there?"

"The answer is simple. You are free in your dreams. You are not tied to reality or to your body. You are almost at the same plane as you are when you are in heaven."

"Does God put messages in our dreams?"

"Yes! Those people who choose to believe, tend to remember their dreams more vividly."

"I remember all my dreams. Sometimes, they seem so real."

"Another reason why you were chosen."

"I just hope I don't let God and you down. I am really enjoying everything right now, and I am afraid it will all be taken away."

"Why are you afraid? God loves you and will always love you."

"I understand that, and I know He loves me and everyone else. I just don't want to fail or make a mistake."

"If you try, you can never fail. Everyone makes mistakes, but it is how you fix your mistake that is important. Remember, even though you are fulfilling some of your own dreams, you are also helping people."

"I hope so. I cannot see what you are seeing, but I trust you and if you say I am helping, I will do what I can to finish my assignment."

"We believe in you as well."

"Thank you! I will do my best."

"We know you will."

"I guess I just don't understand why anyone would turn away from God, but as you said, there are some things I just will not understand."

CHAPTER 12

I learned a lot last night with Andrew, but I needed to shift my focus to baseball. The season would be ending soon, and I knew each time I went to a different sports team, it would be getting more and more difficult. Baseball was a little different. I could not walk down the street like when I was a kid and just jump into a pick-up game at the end of the block. Before I went to try out for football, I called some friends, and we played at the school. With basketball, I just went to the local gym. Baseball would be a little more challenging. I did not have time to start in the minor leagues and I figured I would only get one game like I did in both football and basketball. I sat down to talk to my wife to see if we could figure out the best way to approach this new challenge.

"Hey, Mandy, what do you think is the best way to approach this baseball thing?"

"Why not just go to the ballpark and tell the coach who you are. They should know you by now, and maybe they will be intrigued by your story."

"I never thought of it that way. I think I will do just that. Thank you for your help, for believing in me, and for sticking by me through this. I know it has not been easy."

"You are welcome! I do it because I love you and believe in you."

After that conversation with Mandy, I felt a little better about my baseball assignment. I figured I would just get into the car and drive to the ballpark, just like Mandy said and tell them who I was. What is the worst thing that could happen? Well, I could think of a whole bunch of stuff, but hopefully, everything would work out fine.

I went upstairs to get my stuff. As I packed my gear, I wondered if what I was doing was really making a difference. I was not sure how it could be helping people turn back to God. I started to feel guilty because I was enjoying everything that was happening. At that moment, I fell to my knees and said a prayer to God. I thanked Him for everything that I had, and everything He was doing for me. I told Him I just wished I could sit down and have a conversation with Jesus one day. As much as Andrew said there was a lot I would simply not understand, part of me wanted to. If I could only talk to

Jesus, maybe I could figure out more ways to help. I guess it was that inner self that was trying to get out. Either way, I just wanted to make sure I was doing what I was supposed to do.

As I drove to the ballpark, my thoughts turned back when I was a kid, and how much fun I had playing baseball at the end of my street. We had an island there and it was really easy to mark the bases. In the summer, we would play from morning until night. People just rotated in when they got there and when it was time to leave, someone just took their spot. Baseball gave me a sense of calm. It was not like football and basketball. When I was standing in center field, I had a few moments in between batters to take notice of what I was doing. I never forgot that feeling and was looking forward to it again.

Once I reached the parking lot, I grabbed my bag and headed for the field. I was approached by an older gentleman who stuck out his hand.

"Good morning Daniel. My name is Glenn. I have seen you on TV the last few weeks, and I would like to tell you that I believe you. I believe what is happening to you, and I would like to help."

This took me back a bit.

"Thanks, Glenn! I would like to find a way to try out for the team. I only get to play in one game, but I am not sure how I am going to convince the manager to let me try out."

"I don't think you have to worry about that, Daniel. You see, not only am I a security guard here, I also own the team. Being a security guard allows me to get close to the players, coaches, and fans. Besides, most people do not recognize me. As I said before, I believe in you, and I am going to give you that one game without a try out. I would like you to practice with the team so they get a chance to know you as a person. You have an important job to do, and as I said before, I am here to help."

Was this really happening? I don't need to try out, and I already get my shot. Why would Glenn give me this opportunity? Was it because he really wanted to help or was it because he wanted to win? I am not sure, but I know that I will at least go through with my assignment.

I saw a man talking to a woman who was taking notes. I assumed it was the coach and an assistant. Glenn walked me over to the coach and introduced me.

"Hey Coach Luke, this is Daniel Lavenok. He is here to play baseball. I want you to let him practice with the team a few days and then put him in game four of the series. I have a feeling we are going to help each other."

"Lavenok, did you bring your gear?"

"Yes, Coach!"

"Well, get changed and get out there. Samantha, show him where the locker room is."

With that, I ran into the locker room to change. It was a very large locker room. The walls were a tannish color, and each locker was about as wide as a refrigerator. There was a chair in front for each person. In the middle of the room was a table. I am not sure what that was for, but it was right in the middle. There was an office off the corner with all glass windows. I would assume it was the coach's office. I tried to take a minute to take it all in while I was getting changed. Just as I was in both football and basketball, I became very nervous. I don't care who you are, even if you have the help of God, you are going to get nervous. Several thoughts kept running through my mind. I wondered if I would be able to hit the ball. I would have to use all my skills from when I was a kid as well as all of my brain work for this one. I hung up my stuff and walked over to the mirror. I took a good look at myself and put my hat on. I looked up and asked God to be with me and then took a knee to say a small prayer. When I was done, I started walking toward the field. I could not even see the end of the tunnel because it was so long. As I made my way down the tunnel, Andrew suddenly appeared next to me.

"Hello, Daniel!"

"Hello, Andrew," I said.

"Are you ready for this?"

"I think so. I am just a little nervous. I know you are with me, but I have not stood in a batter's box and starred down a pitcher for a very long time. What if I cannot hit the ball?"

"Daniel, please don't worry about that. Once you step into that box, it will all come back to you. It will be just like your childhood. You will actually feel like you are playing Little League. It is hard to explain, so you will just have to trust me."

"I do, Andrew, but I guess until I get a little confidence, it will be that way."

"I understand. Why don't you go shag some fly balls first! This will help you get your mind set."

"That is a good idea. Will you be on the field?"

"Yes, I will be right behind the batter when you are in the field and right behind the pitcher when you are batting."

"Hey, Andrew, don't I need to be on the roster before the World Series started? I seem to remember that being a rule."

"You let me worry about that, Daniel."

With that, we came to the end of the tunnel, and I ran up the stairs and onto the field. Coach Luke was standing by second base.

"All set, Coach," I said.

"Ok, go shag some flies for a little while. Let's see if you can run a few down."

I was always a good outfielder and could run down most balls. I can only remember one time when I misjudged a ball that came my way. It was from one of the twins back in my early Little League days. That taught me a lesson to always play deep. My father always said it was easier to run in than run out.

I played the outfield for about twenty minutes. Each time a ball came my way, I just let my instincts take over. It was like I was a little kid again. Andrew was right! It was all coming back. I was starting to feel more and more comfortable. I did not miss one fly ball, and it got the attention of the coaches.

"Lavenok, get in here for some batting practice!"

"Yes sir," I said.

I ran over to the dugout and grabbed my gloves out of my back pocket. After trying several bats, I found one I was comfortable with, and put on a helmet. As I walked to the batter's box, I saw Andrew appear behind the pitcher. He had that same smile on his face, and I could hear him in my head.

"Don't worry Daniel. You will do fine," he said.

I walked over to the line and put the bat in between my legs and adjusted my gloves to make them tighter. I squeezed the bat took a deep breath and stepped into the box. It was almost like a time warp, and I was instantly transformed back to my Little League days. I had no fear of the ball coming at me and immediately felt comfortable and ready to swing. As the pitcher took his wind up, I adjusted my back foot and was ready to go. The first pitch that came in was a fastball, and I saw it very clearly. I took a swing and made contact. What I did not expect is for the ball to fly over the fence and into the seats. I guess I surprised myself. Pitch after pitch, the ball came in and, I made great contact. I did not get a home run each time, but I would have been on base each time. This lasted for about ten minutes and then Coach Luke came over.

"Not bad, Lavenok. Do you think you can do the same thing the day after tomorrow? We have a night game, and I would like you start in center field."

"Yes, I do, Coach. I will not let you down."

"Great! Hit the showers, and I will see you in a few days."

As I walked to the locker room to get changed, I tried to take in what just happened to me. I could smell the grass of the ball field. I could imagine what the ballpark would be like with all the fans. I could see myself running around the bases after a home run. I just hoped it all went the way I imagined.

Once I was done, I hopped into my car and began to drive home. I could not wait to get there and tell Mandy about my day. Yes, I could have called her, but it would not be the same as face to face. It was a nice drive from downtown to my house, so I just tried to listen to the radio and take in everything that was happening. It was so amazing; I was even having a hard time believing it was true. As soon as I pulled into the garage, I grabbed my bag from the back seat and headed into the house where Mandy was waiting by the door.

"How did it go?" she asked.

"It was unbelievable. I am not sure I can even put into words what happened. You were right. As I walked up, an older gentleman named Glenn was waiting for me. He said he had seen me on TV and believed in what I was doing and wanted to help. He told me he not only worked there, but was also the owner. He brought me to the coach, and then I did the tryout. It was like I did a time warp and went back to my Little League days. I caught all the balls that came my way and I even ran down a few. The first pitch that I swung at was a home run. After that I hit consistently, and with power. It was simply unbelievable."

"Wow! Sounds pretty incredible. Was Andrew there?"

"Yes, he walked with me in the tunnel on my way to the field, and stayed the whole time."

"What did he say?"

"He basically said that he would be with me and to go out and just relax. I was so nervous for some reason. I trusted him, and once I started to play, I did ok."

"When is the next time you play?"

"I play tomorrow. It is game four of the World Series. They have lost the first three games, and if they lose, the season is over. Hopefully, we can help each other."

"I am sure you will do great. Andrew has never let you down before, and I don't expect him to let you down now."

"Do you only get one game?"

"I think so. I will ask Andrew after the game, but I would assume so."

"After you put your stuff away, your daughter needs your help with some homework."

I put my stuff in the family room and walked over to the kitchen table, sat down next to my daughter, and began to help her with her homework.

CHAPTER 13

I woke up early because I had so much on my mind. I always loved the mornings because it was the start of a new day. In essence, it was a do over and anything I did not do right the day before I could fix. It was also very peaceful and quiet. It gave me a chance to catch up with my thoughts. It also gave me a chance to say thank you to God for all the blessings I have received. I liked to pray when it was quiet. I somehow felt closer to God. I asked Him to please let me do well in the game, and not embarrass myself.

My kids were looking forward to going to the ballpark and seeing a professional game. They were even more excited to see their father play in the game. When I asked them if they understood what was going on, they both said, "Yes." They knew that God was using me to help. They remembered me always telling them that everything happens for a reason. They have learned to trust God through our example. I guess that is what I was showing everyone. I was showing them to trust God through my example, and that of my wife.

After I had breakfast with my family, I told them all goodbye and headed to work. It was a long day and I could not wait to get home. Once I did, I went upstairs to get my stuff. I loaded the car and began my drive to the ballpark. I kept telling myself that this was real. It was not a dream, and it was actually happening. Before I knew it, I was turning into the parking lot of the ballpark. I found a spot where the rest of the players parked and grabbed my stuff. I thought about how this would feel, to be able to do this every day. I stopped where I was and took a knee and looked up to God and said thank you for this opportunity, and for this experience.

As I walked to the locker room, I was getting more and more nervous. Yes, Andrew told me I would do fine, but I was not sure how all the players were going to respond. Who would be sitting out because of me? How would they feel about that? I saw my locker and went to go sit down. A few minutes later, Glenn walked over.

"Hey, Lavenok, I wish you the best of luck out there. I know you will do well. After all, you are doing God's work, so it is impossible not to."

"Thanks, Glenn. I appreciate you believing in me!"

"That is what people are supposed to do. I have owned this team for several years. I have more money than I know what to do with. I set my own schedule and basically do what I want on a daily basis. I get to come to the greatest job in the world, but sometimes, I just don't feel fulfilled. I try to fill that void by doing for others. That is when I feel the best, when I get a chance to help someone else."

"Well, I have to tell you, I was so worried about how I was going to play baseball. You made it much easier than I had expected."

"So, have you talked to God or Jesus?"

"No, but I would love to sit down and have a conversation with Jesus."

"I have asked Andrew if that were possible."

"Who is Andrew?"

"He is the angel who has been helping me."

"I had an experience with an angel once. It changed my life. My brother and I were driving home around 6:30 pm when we saw the car in front of us get hit head on from a drunk driver. I saw a young man come running from his house. It looked as though he knew the people in the car. He seemed to remain calm in this terrible time. I did not understand why until I saw it."

"What did you see, Glenn?"

"I watched this young man hold another young man in his arms and look up. I heard him say to God to please help his friend. As soon as he said that prayer, a very bright light appeared around him. I saw the angel take his wings and wrap it around both of them. They both instantly grew calm, and I felt as though that angel went so deep into his soul to comfort him. It is really hard to explain."

"What happened next?"

"The young man died right there in the arms of his friend. I found out later that it was his best friend. I guess he watched his best friend die that day."

I had chills running up my spine. I immediately knew Glenn had seen me that day. It also confirmed that he saw Andrew.

"Glenn, that was me, holding my best friend. I was the one who looked up and said that prayer. You saw Andrew!"

"I knew there was a special connection with you. I just could not put my finger on it. Thank you for letting me know what really happened. I often think about that accident."

"No, thank you for sharing your story. It means a lot to me to know that someone else has witnessed some of the stuff I have."

"Can I ask you one more thing, Daniel?"

"Sure!"

"Can you win this game? We have never won a game before in the World Series. I don't need to win the whole thing, although I would love that. I just want to win one game. I just want to see what that feels like."

"I will do my best."

With that I grabbed my glove and headed to the tunnel to take batting practice. I was feeling so incredibly excited, it was hard to control my emotions. I had to take a minute to try to relax. Listening to that story from

Glenn really pumped me up. I know it should have depressed me, but just knowing that someone else witnessed what happened gave me something I had not had in a while – HOPE!

I took batting practice and caught some fly balls and headed to the dugout for the start of the game.

Playing professional baseball was nothing like anything I could have imagined. As we were taking batting practice, the crowd started filling in. They would watch us hit as well as field fly balls. Some players would walk over and sign autographs while others would pose for pictures. It seemed like every minute, more and more people were entering the ballpark. The announcer introduced a local police officer to throw out the first pitch, and then we all stood for the national anthem. Once I hear this song, it helps to get me ready to play. I would always make sure it was sung or played at all of my games when I was coaching. It was the least I could do to honor the men and women who serve this country.

Coach Luke called us over, told us to go out, and take the game. We huddled up, did a cheer, and ran onto the field. What an unbelievable scene it was! As I jogged to center field, I saw the crowd stand up and start cheering.

It was so loud; I could barely hear anything. It took a while, but I finally found Mandy and the kids. They were just behind third base, a little to the right, about a third of the way up. She smiled at me, and I was ready to play.

I saw Andrew right behind home plate. He gave me his usual smile and pointed toward right center. I guess he gave me a heads up because the batter hit the ball in that exact direction. I ran over made the catch and threw the ball in. After the third out was made, I ran into the dugout and sat down. I was batting sixth and could not wait until it was my turn. The first two batters got on base, but the next two got out. I grabbed my helmet and went to the on-deck circle. I took a couple practice swings and wondered if I would be batting with the bases loaded. Knowing my luck, that is exactly what I expected to happen. Once the ump called ball four, I knew it was really happening.

"Now batting, number 13 – Daniel Lavenok," the announcer said.

I slowly walked over to the batter's box and tried to take it all in. I looked down to the third base coach who gave me the signs. I had the green light to swing away. I adjusted my gloves, took a tight grip on the bat, took a deep breath, and stepped into the batter's box. I figured the first pitch would be a fastball so I was ready to take a swing. I used to be a first ball hitter when I played Little League. The pitcher took his wind up, and threw the ball. I swung and made contact. The ball went to deep left center field and rolled to the wall. I sprinted towards first base and continued to second. I noticed the left fielder was just getting to the ball and figured I could make it to third. I hit the bag on the inner corner and tried to get the triple. I went in head first and beat the throw. I had just hit a triple and knocked in three runs. We were up 3-0.

"Hell of a hit, Lavenok," said Coach Luke.

"Thanks, Coach," I replied.

Every time we scored, they scored. It was now the fourth inning, and I was coming to bat. There were two guys on, and I was hoping to get another hit. I was ready for the first pitch fastball again. I was right! It came in, I swung, and it went over the centerfielder's head. I rounded first and headed to second. I did another head first slide and beat the tag. Another two runs came in. We were now up 6-4. I made some more catches in center and the game continued on. It was now the seventh inning, and I was leading off. Would the pitcher send me that first pitch fastball again? I was not sure, but I was going to swing. It came in pretty fast, I leaned back and took my swing. It was a solid hit to right field. I ran to first and waited to be brought home. The next two batters struck out. With two outs, I figured I would never get a chance to score a run, but that changed when Rexer hit a double to the wall. I sprinted around the bases and the third base coach was waiving me home. I made it no problem.

"Hey, Lavenok, how do you feel?"

"Pretty good Glenn. Why do you ask?"

"I think something special is going to happen, and we are going to win this game."

"Like what?"

"Do you even realize what you have done so far?"

"Sure, I have three hits and five RBI's."

"You have a triple, double, and a single. All you need is a home run to hit the cycle. Did you know it has never been done before in the World Series?"

"No! I guess I was not really paying attention to that."

"I think you are going to hit for the cycle, and you are going to hit the game winning home run?"

"What makes you say that?"

"Because of that!"

He had this weird look on his face when he pointed out towards center field. There was Andrew standing on the warning track.

"Glenn, can you see him?"

"Yes! I can see him. It is the same angel I saw so many years ago at the accident. I know we are going to win this game."

A single tear came down the right side of his cheek. He leaned over and gave me a hug and said, "Thank you!"

"I have not done anything yet."

"You have done more than you know."

It was now the bottom of the ninth, and the game was tied. I would be batting third this inning. I figured we would get at least one base runner, and I would drive him in and we would win the game. However, that did not happen. I was in the on-deck circle when I thought about what Glenn had said. "I don't want to make the last out. I hate when I have to make the last out."

"Who says you are going to make the last out?" a voice said in my head.

"Nice to hear from you, Andrew."

"You have done this before, and you can do it again, Daniel."

I knew what he was talking about. I had hit the game winning home run back in ninth grade. It was a great feeling, and something I would love to do again, but this was the World Series. As I walked up to the plate, the manager of the other team came out to switch pitchers. He called for the lefty, and boy was he big! He came out of the bullpen and I just looked at him in awe. I watched him warm up. He was a fantastic pitcher. He was about 6' 7" and threw a 100-mph fastball. I watched Andrew appear on the mound, and I was able to hear their conversation.

"What do you want to do with him, Phil?"

"I want to pitch to him. I can get him out."

"Do you know who he is?"

"Yes, I know who he is.   He is the one from the papers.   He just got done playing football and basketball.   I know he said he is doing God's work, but I think that is a bunch of crap!   I think he just got lucky and I am going to be the one who spoils his baseball outing."

"Ok, Phil.  I hope you know what you are doing."

With that, the coach left the mound, and Phil took off his hat, wiped his face, and put the hat back on.   I tightened my gloves and stepped into the box.   I knew he would not be giving me a first pitch fastball.   He was watching the game.   He took his wind up and threw the first pitch. It was a curve ball.

"Striiiiiike," yelled the ump.

I stepped out of the box, fixed my gloves, took a deep breath, and stepped back in.   The next pitch came in, and it was a fastball.   I took a good rip, but fouled it off because it came in so fast.   "Ok, two strikes, and now I am in the hole," I thought.

The crowd was now standing.   The noise was incredible. They were cheering and clapping, hoping for some sort of miracle play. Phil walked off the mound, and took off his hat. He slowly, and meticulously put it back on, and stepped onto the mound. He shrugged off all the signs, and I knew Phil would be bringing the heat again, but this time I was ready. I took a deep breath, and asked for God's help! He went through his wind up, and on his release, I saw the ball very clearly. I took my swing, and I watched the ball hit my bat. I knew I made good contact, and I was right. I started to run to first, but could not take my eye of the ball. It was on its way over the left field fence. I had done it! I had hit a home run, and we won the game 8-7. The crowd went nuts. The players stormed onto the field. It was crazy! I remember taking my time while I ran around the bases. I could see Mandy in the stands clapping with my family as I approached third base. I turned the corner, and headed for home. Andrew was there, and he gave me a big smile. The whole team was waiting for me. I touched home plate and ended the game.

"Holy crap! Did that just happen?" I said to Glenn.

"You bet it did. Thank you, Lavenok! Thank you!"

## CHAPTER 14

When I got to the locker room, I was too excited to do anything. I just sat by my locker and began to pray. I thanked God for everything, and I hoped that I was doing what I was supposed to be doing. After about ten minutes, I showered and headed to the press conference. I was not sure how this one would go, but I was ready.

As I approached the podium, my favorite reporter was there and had to ask the first question.

"Hello, Joshua. What is your question?"

"I want to know what is going on and don't give me the - I am doing God's work stuff."

"I am sorry, Joshua, was there a question in that?"

"Lavenok, I guess I could understand you doing well in football and maybe even in basketball. But, to do what you are doing in three different professional sports is highly unlikely unless you are doing something different. My question is, what type of drug are you on?"

"As I told you before, I am not on any drugs. I was approached by an angel, and I am doing God's work."

"Yeah, yeah. The standard answer. Seriously, that is really going to be your answer all the time?"

"It is the truth! Why do you always think I have something to hide? Why is it so hard to believe that God is with us?"

"Because what you are doing is not possible, yet you are doing it."

"Joshua, can we talk after the press conference? This way, other people may ask their questions."

"Sure, I will meet you in the parking lot."

Most of the other questions were pretty standard. How did you feel after you hit the home run? Why can you only play one game? What are your plans? I tried to answer each question to the best of my ability, and everyone there seemed to accept what I was saying, except for Joshua. After the press conference, I found Mandy and the kids. We talked for a little while, and they told me how proud they were of me. Not just for winning the game, but also, for doing God's work. It meant a lot to them that I was trying to do the right thing. I told Mandy and the kids that I would be home after meeting with Joshua.

"Sorry Mandy, but if I don't go meet Joshua, he will just keep showing up. I hope we have a good conversation."

"I am sure you will and just remember to be yourself."

"Thanks Mandy! See you soon."

With that Mandy and the kids left, and I went to meet Joshua. He was waiting by my car.

"Hello Joshua. Would you like to talk here or go somewhere else?"

"Can we go to the diner around the corner?"

"Sure, I will meet you there in five minutes."

He turned around to find his car, and I got into my car and started to drive to the diner. It was a nice quiet place. I was just worried how this interview was going to go. For all I knew, he would be recording the whole thing.

"Over here, Lavenok," he said.

"Thank you for meeting me, Josh. May I call you Josh?"

"Sure, that is fine."

"I am just curious why you have it out for me? Why do you think I am doing something wrong?"

"Lavenok, I have been a reporter for over twenty years. I know when something is not right, and I can smell that there is something not right with this whole story."

"Ok, since you don't believe any of my answers, what do you suggest?"

"How about I ask you one question? I would like you to think about it and then give me your answer. If it is good enough, I will give you the week off, or until I see you at the news conference of your next sport."

"Sure, go ahead. Ask away."

I figured it would be something similar to the many questions he asked at the news conferences, but what he asked me totally threw me for a loop.

"Lavenok, you get to time travel.  You can go anywhere you want, but you can only go for fifteen minutes.  You can go anywhere in the future or anywhere in the past."

"Anywhere in the future or anywhere in the past?  Is this my past or future or any past or future?"

"It is not specifically your past or future."

"Wow, I must say your question threw me a little off guard.  That is a very difficult question.  How long do I get to think about it?"

"You get five minutes, starting now!"

This was a very interesting question.  What answer did I think Joshua was looking for?  Maybe he wanted me to say the future to see what was happening, but I knew in my heart what I really wanted to say.  I could hear Mandy saying to be myself.  Just be honest, so that is what I was going to do.  I was not going to say what I thought he wanted to hear, but rather just give him my answer and not worry about what he thought.

"Times up.  Where is it going to be?"

"If I only get one choice, I would choose the past. I would like to meet Jesus."

"Ok, now your answer totally surprised me. Why would you want to do that? Why would you not want to go into the future to see what your life would be like or go way into the future to see your kids? Better yet, why would you not go into the future one week and get the lotto numbers and become a millionaire?"

"I guess none of that matters to me. I think Ralph Waldo Emerson said it better than I ever could. He said, "What lies behind us and what lies before us are tiny matters compared to what lies within us." I have learned from my past. Would I like to change some of it, you bet, but it has made me who I am today. Would I love to know the future, sure, but I know God has a plan for me, and I have learned to trust Him. So, what lies within me is to see and have a conversation with Jesus."

"I guess I did not expect that kind of an answer. Thank you, Lavenok."

"Wait, are you quoting me on that?"

"You bet!   Why?  Are you afraid of what people might think?"

"No, feel free to quote any of that as long as you do it correctly.   I have nothing to hide and that is how I feel."

"Great, I will be putting this on the front page of the sports page."

"That is swell, Josh.  I look forward to reading it."

He took one last sip of his coffee, grabbed his notebook, and was on his way.   I sat there wondering if what just happened was going to hurt or help.   I was not sure, but I know Andrew would know, so I left some money on the table and headed for my car.   It would be an interesting drive home.   As soon as I got to my car, Andrew was waiting for me.

"Hi Andrew.  Did you hear the interview?"

"Yes, I did, Daniel."

"Did I make a mistake?"

"Why would you say that?"

"I don't know.  Maybe I gave the wrong answer."

"Did you tell the truth?"

"Yes!"

"Then you can never give the wrong answer. Let me give you a few words of wisdom."

"Great, I could use some right now."

"Life is not about getting or holding all the best cards. It is about playing the cards you have."

"Great quote, I have heard it before, but how does this relate to what we are talking about?"

"Daniel, people who are too weak to follow their own dreams will always find a way to discourage yours."

"Ok, another great quote, but I am not following you this time."

"Ok, my fault. Everyone in life has a purpose. Do you remember that?"

"Yes, of course!"

"One of the reasons you were chosen was because of your experiences – your cards. You have played them well. You have found several people that have tried to get you off your path, but you leaned on God and found your way back. You were strong enough to follow your own dreams. Making a little more sense now?"

"Yes, I get it now. Whatever life has dealt me; I have found a way to deal with it. I have also, with my faith in God, found a way to move past the negative people in my life to get where I am right now.

"You got it, Daniel!"

"Thank you once again, Andrew. I am human remember. I need a little explaining once in a while."

"That is what I am here for. Now, we have one more sport to go. Fortunately, there is a game that you will be playing in very soon. The season is just getting under way, and an old friend will be there to help you."

"An old friend?"

"Yes, an old friend. Just show up to the arena, and you will be all set."

"Ok, Andrew, I will see you tomorrow."

Once he left, I pulled into the garage and headed into to see my wife and kids.

## CHAPTER 15

After a good night's sleep, I felt ready to take on the day. I was not a very good sleeper because I just can't shut off my brain sometimes. When I wake up, I always have to check on the kids, and by the time I get back in bed, I am thinking of all the stuff I did not finish, or all the stuff I have to start. My mind is going a million miles an hour. However, knowing that I was not imagining Andrew and having a guardian angel made me sleep a little better. As I walked downstairs to breakfast, Mandy asked me how I slept.

"How did you sleep?"

"Ok, you?"

"Ok. What are you going to do about hockey? I know the season just started, so hopefully, they will give you a chance."

"I am not sure, but for some reason, I am just not worried about it. I think I will just go to the arena and see what happens. What do you think?"

"I think that is a good plan."

After breakfast, I said goodbye to Mandy and the kids and headed downtown to the hockey arena. I asked Andrew to be with me as I approached the parking lot, but what happened next, shocked even me.

"Hello, Daniel," the man said.

"Hello," I said back. "How do you know me?"

"Seriously! Anyone who watches the news knows who you are. You are doing God's work, and I am here to help. My name is George, and my brother told me you would be coming."

"Brother?"

"Yes, my brother Glenn. Did he not tell you that we own both the baseball and hockey teams?"

"I think he forgot to mention that."

"Well, my brother and I received a very large inheritance when we were young, but could not touch any of the money until we got our education. Once we both graduated, we went into business together. We tried a whole bunch of things, but found that we both loved sports so we looked at owning a team. Several years ago, we had the opportunity to buy both teams, and we just did it. That is how G and G holdings came about."

"I knew someone bought the teams, but I was not sure who?"

"Well that was us. We own both teams together, but Glenn likes baseball, and I like hockey, so we get a chance to be in the sport we love."

"That sounds simple enough. Tell me, George, did you have an encounter with an angel too?"

"Do you remember when Glenn told you about driving home with his brother and seeing an accident?"

"That, was you?"

"Yes!"

"Ok, makes sense now. Did he tell you about our conversation?"

"Yes, he told me all about it, especially the part about you being the person that watched his best friend die. We have not spoken about it for years, but when you came into our lives, it helped to heal an old wound."

"I am glad that I was able to help."

"Come on, I will show you where the locker room is. We have a game in a few hours, and you will be playing in it."

"What?" I said.

"Our goalie went down last night, so I will just tell everyone we signed you to a one-day contact. It should not be an issue, but we are playing the defending Stanley Cup Champions tonight. It is a sell out, so is should be exciting."

"George, you have to excuse me. I need to call my wife and let her know what is going on."

"Sure, take your time. I will be right here."

I called Mandy and let her know what was happening. She promised to bring the kids and the rest of my family and meet me at the arena before the game. I told her I loved her and thanked her for being flexible. Once I was finished, I found George, and we went into the locker room. He introduced me to Coach John.

"Hey, Coach John. This is Lavenok, and he is your new goalie for tonight."

"Lavenok, ever played goalie before?"

"Yes, I played in gym class in high school."

"George, is this some kind of joke?"

"John, you and I have always had a good relationship. You have learned to trust me, and I have learned to trust you over the years. This is one of those times where you trust me and just say ok."

"Ok, George, I will trust you, but if we get blown out, it is on you."

"No problem, John. I will even take the mic and apologize to all the fans after the game if that happens."

I was just standing there listening to George and John talk about me. I began to get a little nervous. I was feeling fine before, but now George was putting a little pressure on me.

"Go get dressed, Lavenok. When you are done, I will introduce you to the guys."

Once I finished getting dressed, Coach John began his game speech.

"I know the season just started, and we are already being tested. We lost Baker for a few days to a shoulder injury, but we need to leave our worrying here. Once we step out on that ice, it will be in God's hands. Just go out and play the way I know you can play and regardless of what the score is at the end, you should be happy with the results. You are a great group of guys, and you look out for each other. Just keep doing what you are doing. Oh, this is, Lavenok, he will be in goal tonight. Let's get out there and get this win!"

I was excited, but also very nervous. I had not put on a pair of skates for at least ten years. I was an ok skater, but there was no way I could compete with these guys. While we were walking out of the tunnel, I called for Andrew. He appeared right at the end.

"Andrew, I am a little nervous. I have never come down and played a game right away like this. I am not a great skater, and I am sure I am going to mess up. What do I do?"

"Daniel, please don't worry. I am with you. Just go out and put yourself in goal. Every time a shot is taken, you will see the puck very clearly. You will be able to use your instincts and athletic ability to stop every shot taken."

"But what if I can't?"

"You will. Have we let you down before?"

"No, but I played football, basketball, and baseball. I did not play a lot of hockey, but I trust you completely."

"Thank you, Daniel. I need to remember that you are human, and you need a little reassurance once in a while. Are you ready?"

"Yes, thank you, Andrew."

As I took off my skate covers, I saw Mandy and the kids. They were right behind the bench. She just gave me her usual look, and I felt more at ease. I stepped out onto the ice and skated toward the goal. I have watched enough hockey that I know what to do, but the goalie can make or break the game. I just did not want to let anyone down.

"Hey, Lavenok, I hate losing, so how about you do a good job tonight," Stenchem said in a somewhat broken accent.

"You bet! Just keep them off me, and we will be fine."

He skated away, and we all stood for the national anthem. Once that was over, Stenchem and Sambren squared up for the face off. The puck was dropped, and the game was under way. It was very stressful being in goal. The game moved so fast, and I had a hard time keeping an eye on the puck. Whoever said being a goalie was easy was wrong. We kept moving the puck into their zone; they kept bringing it into our zone. But no shots were taken. Then it happened, there was a breakaway, and Sarlia had the puck and was heading my way. He put on a fake and took a shot to the upper left corner. I snatched it into my glove and threw it back out for Stenchem. The game went on like this for a while, and each time a shot was taken, I stopped it. I could see the puck very clearly. It was almost like the puck was the size of a small tire. We ended up scoring and took the lead into the third period. Shot after shot, I was stopping everything, even when we were trying to fight off a power play. I had already stopped 24 shots. There were only five minutes left in the game, and we had a 1-0 lead. I knew the other team would be coming at us with everything they had. It did not matter. I was able to stop every shot, and the game ended. We had won!

After we shook hands and headed off the ice, I saw Stenchem.

"Hey, Lavenok, nice job! You can goal for us anytime. Anyone who can shut out the defending Stanley Cup Champions, is ok in my book."

"Thanks, man. I appreciate it," I said.

I went over to my locker and just sat and tried to reflect on what just happened. Better yet, I asked myself if it really did happen. I was interrupted by George.

"Hey, Lavenok, nice game."

"Thanks, George, I surprised myself."

"How are you going to handle the press conference?"

"I am not sure, why? Do you have a good idea?"

"No, I just was wondering. I have a feeling Josh will be up to his old tricks."

"I hope not. He asked me if I would rather go into the future or into the past. I gave him my answer, and he told me he would give me a break with some time off, so hopefully, he will be fine."

"Let's hope so, but I would not hold your breath."

"I guess we will see what happens."

I showered and headed to the press conference where I was sure something exciting was waiting for me.

## CHAPTER 16

As I walked out to the podium, it was a pretty big crowd. I saw all the usual people, including Joshua. It was very weird because Joshua did not ask the first question.

"Hey, Lavenok, what was it like to be in goal?"

"It was great, but a little terrifying at the same time. That puck moves pretty fast. As time went on, I became a little more comfortable and a little more confident."

"Hey, Lavenok, how did it feel to beat the defending Stanley Cup Champions?"

"How do you think it feels? It feels pretty great!"

"Hey, Lavenok, why do you always have number 13 on your jersey? What is the significance of that number?"

"You are probably going to think it is crazy, but there is Jesus, and then there were twelve apostles, hence, thirteen."

"Interesting! Thank you for explaining."

It was a pretty normal press conference, and most of the remaining questions were just your standard questions. That is until it was Joshua's turn.

"Hey, Lavenok, can you tell all of us about your brain research? I think many of us here would really like to know about it."

"What would you like to know?"

"I understand you did some pretty intensive research, and you made a breakthrough. Can you tell us about it?"

"Sure! I have always believed that we could use more of our brain in our everyday lives, so I did research on how to use more of your brain."

"Can you be a little more specific? How much Adderall and sugar do you mix?"

How in the hell did he know that? I never told anyone about my research except my wife and Andrew. They were the only two other people who would know. I knew that neither one of them would tell, so how did he know? I wondered if he followed me or broke into my house. How would I answer this? I began to panic, and I looked around for Andrew. He was standing in the back and told me to answer truthfully.

"I figured that the brain could be trained just like muscles could. Take geese for example. Basically, whatever living creature a gosling sees upon hatching, that is larger than itself, it thinks it is that species. This is called imprinting. What if this could be done in the human brain? What if we could alter parts of the brain that were used for specific functions? I knew that there were specific drugs that worked in changing the chemical balance of the brain, so I focused on all the ADHD and ADD medications. There were so many to choose from, but in the end, I decided on Adderall. Not only was it a performance enhancer, and a cognitive enhancer, it increased the activity of my neurotransmitters. My results lasted only four to six hours and the side effects were minimal. I also figured that if I put it in sugar and drank it, I would get the most benefit because sugar acts as a great transport. I also used the lowest strength there was and kept adjusting until I found the right dosage."

"What results are you talking about?"

By now, the crowd was making noise and some of them started to scream "CHEATER – LAVENOK IS A CHEATER!"

The jeering came from everywhere. Most of the people in the room were screaming that I was a cheater.

"I am not a cheater. Let me explain!"

It was no use, people started to come after me, and they were pretty damn mad. I was so upset with Joshua I lost my temper and went after him. The security guards had to separate us. "What a jerk," I thought. He told me that he would take it easy on me if I answered his question about the future or past, and he came after me. I hope I don't meet him in an alley somewhere because I will kick his butt!

After being escorted from the press conference, the security guards brought me to the holding area away from the crowds. George was there and told me that he still believed in me.

"Hey, Lavenok, there is no way you could have done those things without the help of God or angels. I don't care what Joshua says. It does not matter to me."

"Thank you, George! That means a lot to me. I am beginning to question everything myself."

After driving home and really having time to think, I walked into the house and saw Mandy.

"Well, that was interesting," she said.

"Yeah, I don't do anything half-assed. Unfortunately, I am not sure how this is going to turn out now."

"Why don't you go talk to Andrew and see what he has to say."

"Ok, I will be back in a bit."

I walked over to the den, and Andrew was already there waiting for me.

"What the heck happened back there Andrew?"

"I am not sure, Daniel. Maybe this is some sort of test!"

"Haven't I been tested enough? What possible test could this be?"

"For we are God's workmanship, created in Christ Jesus, to do good works, which God prepared in advance for us to do. This is from Ephesians 2:10"

"You lost me! Sorry, Andrew."

"Daniel, what do you think that means?"

"I don't know, maybe that God wants us to do good things."

"Not a bad guess, Daniel. Yes, God made you from nothing, and yes, He wants you to do good things. He also wants you to understand salvation. You see, Jesus died on the cross for our sins, and all any of us have to do is just ask Him for forgiveness. We all have the opportunity to enter heaven. You do not have to wait until you get to heaven to do good work. We all have the choice to do it now. Daniel, people will always remember those that have helped them, just as you will remember those that have helped you."

"So, you are saying that if I have done something wrong in my life, all I need to do is ask for forgiveness, and I will go to heaven."

"Yes, Daniel. That is what I am saying. Ask Jesus to come into your life."

"Is it really that simple?"

"Why wouldn't it be? People judge, God does not judge. Remember we talked about that?"

"I remember, but what does that have to do with me, or what we have been doing these past few months? I don't see any kind of connection."

"Everything happens for a reason, Daniel. Sometimes, you just don't understand why."

"Yeah, yeah, I remember, but I like to understand, especially when it is about doing something for God. I don't want to fail, Andrew."

"Daniel, you have not failed, but I feel you may be having one more test. It is going to test your faith this time. I hope you are ready."

"Ohhhh, I think I am ready. Just tell me what I have to do."

"I am afraid you are going to have to make the choice this time. We will be with you, but the decision will be yours."

Andrew turned around and disappeared. I wondered what he meant by this. Our whole conversation was somewhat confusing for me so I tried to replay it over and over in my head. I wanted to understand. After about an hour, I headed upstairs to talk to Mandy.

CHAPTER 17

I did not sleep well and was up early going over everything that had happened yesterday. It was so much to comprehend. Hoping to clear my mind a little, I went outside to get the paper. I closed the door behind me and laid the paper on the island. I fed the animals and made myself a cup of tea. It was a nice morning. I could see the sun just beginning to rise. I opened the door leading to my deck, and I could hear the birds singing, yet it was so quiet. I began to relax a little. I started to think about all that I had. I was happily married, with two great kids. I had a job I loved, and I was doing God's work. My mood started to change, and I thought to myself that it did not matter what other people thought. I was not a cheater. I was doing what I was told, and if people did not choose to believe me, then that was their problem. Andrew had warned me about this way before we started this journey.

I was skimming through the paper when I reached the sports section. That is when my day was ruined. Right there on the front page was a picture of me from each of the four sports. They were action shots lined up next to each other going across the top of the page. The title of the article said, "Angels or Virtual Visions?  You decide!"

I proceeded to read the article and became more infuriated as I read it.

"Are angels real?  Did Lavenok deceive all of us?  Why did they choose him?  Will we ever know?  I have been a reporter for years, and I have never seen anything like this before.  Here is a man who was an average person.  He has a good job, a family, has no criminal record, etc.  He is just an average typical everyday person.  All of a sudden, an angel appears to him and asks him to do God's work.  Why him?  Why not me?  Why not any of you?  He tells him he is going to get special powers to play four professional sports and will succeed far beyond athletes that have been playing professionally for years.  How is this possible?  Do you really believe that it is an angel?  Anything is possible, but it is also highly unlikely that Lavenok was able to do this without tapping into some kind of brain altering drug.  I think he found a way to manipulate his brain so he is getting full use out of it.  There was a movie about this.  The man took a pill and was able to tap into the full potential of his brain.  Lavenok did the same thing except he found a way not only to alter his mind, but also his athletic ability. In short, you could say he is on steroids without the steroids. I think he should share this with us before it gets into the wrong hands. Can you imagine what would happen if another country were to get hold of this technology? Personally, I think he is full of crap, a liar, a cheat, and has fooled us all. If you agree with me, I think you should let him know how you feel the next time you see him."

I almost choked on my food while I was reading. Oh man, was I angry. I told Mandy I was going to get into the car and go find Joshua. She told me to take a breath and calm down.

"I don't want to bail you out of jail today. Can you please use the 24-hour rule?"

"Yes, I will try!"

Mandy was usually the only person that could get through to me, and I knew she was right, so I tried to put down the paper and finish my breakfast. It did not last long because the phone started to ring off the hook. Messages started to come in and I was having a hard time hearing them.

"Lavenok, you are a liar. What a great example you are for our kids!"

"Lavenok, cheaters go to hell!"

"I hope you drive your car off a cliff."

"Hey Lavenok, I believe you..........just kidding. Why don't you go kill yourself!"

Seriously, this was really making me angry, and I wanted to lash out at everyone, but I remembered that Andrew said I would be having one more test. I am sure this is it. How would I react to this? I stopped for a minute and really thought about what was really going on. Maybe these people are just jealous. Maybe they had a bad day. Maybe they are just jerks. Either way, I was not going to play their game. I figured I would just stay quiet for a few days. However, as I read the last paragraph in the article, I knew I could not stay quiet.

"I have a proposal for Lavenok, and I hope he is reading this. How can we show that he is really doing God's work, and it is not the brain research? I think I have an answer, but he would have to agree to it, so here is my proposal. Even if you have altered your brain, we need to find a test that takes your brain altering drug out of the equation. You have played four professional sports, but anyone may have gotten lucky. I would like to see you run the mile, however, if you really want me to believe that you have the intervention of an angel, you need to run it in under four minutes. If you do this successfully, you will not only have me believe, but you will also be the oldest person to run a mile in under four minutes. If you accept this challenge, I will contact you, and we can meet. There will be no cameras, no other spectators, and we will run at a place of my choosing."

Wow! I thought I was angry before. I was furious now! Joshua was such a pain in the neck. I wondered what I had done to him to make him come after me like that.

"Maybe he is just looking for the next big story," Mandy said.

"I don't know, but he is really pissing me off. I just want to find this guy and hit him."

"And, what would that solve?"

"It would make me feel better!"

"For how long? Really? How old are you?"

"Ok, you are right, but that doesn't mean that I can't be pissed at him."

"So, what are you going to do?"

"I am going to call him and accept his challenge. Why, what do you think I should do?"

"I agree with you. Call him and see what he wants you to do."

I thought for a few minutes about what I was going to say to Joshua. I was afraid I was going to scream at him on the phone. So, I fell to my knees and began to pray.

"Lord, Andrew, if either of you can hear me, please help guide my conversation with Joshua. I know you have always been with me, but somehow, this feels different. I am asking for your help. I am thankful for what has happened, but I just want to see this through and finish strong. I ask this in Jesus' name. Amen!"

I had called for Andrew after that, but he did not show up. I wondered why, but maybe this was part of the test. Maybe I just needed to believe everything would be ok.

I picked up the phone and dialed Joshua's number.

"Hello, Daniel," he said.

"Hello, Joshua"

"So, I am assuming you read my article and would like to take my challenge."

"Yes! Just name the time and place, and I will be there."

"Tomorrow at 9:00 a.m. I will meet you at your son's high school. Please come alone and be ready to run."

"I will see you then."

"And, Daniel?"

"Yes, Joshua?"

"I hope you are ready because you have no idea what is about to happen. Nooooo idea!"

I thought that was kind of a strange way to end the conversation, but everything was all messed up anyway. Andrew had said those exact words to me the first night he revealed himself to me. Was this a coincidence? I guess I would find out soon enough. I told Mandy about my conversation with Joshua. Then, I finished my schoolwork, said good night to the kids and headed up to bed. Mandy was waiting for me.

"You ok?" she said.

"Yes! It was kind of weird. Joshua said the exact same thing Andrew said when he first revealed himself to me. He said, "I hope you are ready because you have no idea what is about to happen. Nooooo idea!"

"I am not sure I know what that means, if anything."

"I would not worry about it. Just get a good night's sleep. It is going to be a busy day tomorrow."

"Ok, but I can't stop thinking about it."

We said good night to each other, and I said some more prayers before I drifted off to sleep.

# CHAPTER 18

I woke up early because I could not sleep. I kept thinking about what Joshua had said. Why would he say the exact same thing as Andrew? Did he know Andrew? Something just did not seem right. I went about doing my normal routine and got ready to leave. Mandy came down and asked how I felt.

"I am ok," I replied.

"Do you think you can break four minutes?"

"I don't know, but I will give it my best shot. I don't think Andrew would do all this and then have me fail. He has not let me down before."

"Speaking of Andrew, have you seen or talked to him?"

"No! I wonder why he is not answering."

"Well, good luck today and let me know if you need anything."

"Thank you, Mandy. I love you!"

"Love you too!"

I gave her a kiss and walked out to the garage. I jumped into my car and drove off to the high school. As I pulled into the parking lot, I noticed that it was totally empty. There was no one there. Joshua was already waiting by the track. It seemed kind of strange that on a Saturday morning at 9:00 a.m. there was not one person, one activity or anything else going on. I mean the place was completely empty. Not one car was in the parking lot. Again, I got this feeling that something was just not right.

"Good morning, Joshua," I said.

"Good morning, Daniel! Are you ready?"

"I will give it my best shot."

Not much conversation took place after that, which was fine with me. It took everything I had not to walk up to him and let him have it. I just tried to clear my mind and focus on the task at hand. It was a very quiet morning, eerily quiet. It was about 68°, and there was absolutely no wind. It seemed like the perfect morning to run. I walked over to the bench, set my stuff down, and began to warm up. I slowly jogged on the track and then began to stretch. I said a silent prayer.

"Lord, please let me do this for you. I have worked so hard to do what I was asked. Please let my feet move quickly and my legs feel light as a feather. I ask this in Jesus' name. Amen."

"You ready, Lavenok?"

"Yes, I am ready, Joshua."

"May your feet move quickly, and your legs feel light as a feather."

"What the hell," I thought? Joshua looked at me with this strange smile as I walked over to the starting line.

"Anytime you are ready, just start running, and I will start timing."

I looked up one more time and asked God to be with me, and I started to run. As I rounded the first turn, I felt pretty good. I was running a pretty decent pace. I just tried to keep my stride and focus on running, but my mind started to wander about everything that was happening. Before I knew it, I had completed the first lap. As I continued to run I could feel myself begin to get into a rhythm. My legs and arms were working perfectly together as I ran. I completed the second lap and was now on to the third. I was thinking I was running at least a sixty second quarter. This would be perfect so I could just sprint at the end to beat the four-minute mark. As I began the fourth and final lap, I had all kinds of images flashing in my head. I started to think about the first time I saw Andrew. I was thinking about all that was said, and the awesome experiences I had with each of the four sports teams. This inspired me to give it my all, and I began to sprint with about 200 meters left. As I rounded the final turn, I was feeling pretty good and just gave it everything I had. I crossed the finish line and literally fell to the ground. I had nothing left to give. I was completely exhausted. After about ten minutes, I got up and walked over to Joshua.

"So, what was my time?"

"I am afraid you did not meet your goal. You ran a great race, but a far cry from the four-minute mark."

"What was my time?"

"5:23"

"What!" I exclaimed.

"Daniel, you did not break four minutes. I am sorry."

"Well, I guess you were right Joshua. You win! Feel free to publish whatever you want. That was the agreement."

"That is all you have to say?"

"What do you want me to say?" I turned and yelled. "I am starting to doubt myself."

I grabbed my stuff from the bench and started to walk away. I mumbled under my breath to Andrew.

"Andrew, I don't understand. Where were you? How could you let Joshua win? He is such a jerk. God, I am so angry."

"I am not a jerk, and Andrew is right here," I heard Joshua scream.

I stopped in my tracks, but did not turn around. Now, I was totally freaked out. There was absolutely no way Joshua could have heard me from where he was standing. I slowly turned around and began walking back to the track. As I approached Joshua, he had this funny smile on his face.

"Can you please tell me how you heard what I said? Can you explain your comment about having no idea what was about to happen?"

"I am not who you think I am!" he said.

"I am beginning to realize that."

Joshua looked at me like Andrew did the first time I met him. I felt his gaze go deep into my soul, and I felt a tremendous warmth, like nothing I have ever felt before. It was then I saw his face begin to change. It was slowly morphing. I watched a beard and moustache begin to grow on his face. His hair began to grow, and his eyes became the most piercing blue you could ever imagine. It was then I realized who I was speaking to. It was Jesus!

"Oh, my God," I exclaimed!

"No, that would be my Father!"

I fell to my knees and begged Jesus to forgive me for all the awful things I had said and thought about him.

"There is no need to apologize, Daniel. You said those things about Joshua, not me. Please stand up."

"I probably should not have said them at all, but you, or he, made me so angry."

"You are human. It is ok! I bet you are probably wondering what is happening?"

"Yes, I am!"

"At least you now understand my comment about what was about to happen, and how I heard your mumbling to Andrew."

"Yeah, I kind of figured that out."

"Daniel, I want you to do me a favor please."

"Sure, anything you need."

"I want you to run the mile again."

"Wait, what? Did you say you wanted me to run the mile again? Now?"

"Yes, and this time, I want you to put all your trust in me and just run. Can you do that for me?"

"Yes, but I am exhausted. I have nothing left."

"Trust Me, Daniel."

"Ok, Jesus!"

I walked over to the bench and set my stuff down and began to warm up.

"There is no need for any warmup, Daniel. Just start running," Jesus said.

"Ok."

I began to run my second mile, but something was different this time. I felt as though I was running in some kind of time warp. I swear everything around me went from being clear to blurry to clear again. As I rounded the second turn, I felt really good. As I finished my first lap, I saw both Jesus and Andrew standing next to the finish line. I continued to run and was not even winded. How could I run a mile a little while ago, be totally exhausted to the point where I could not even get up for ten minutes, and now run like I was possessed? It was the strangest feeling, and I doubt I would ever have this feeling again. I continued to run and again, got into a nice rhythm. In the final lap, I saw Andrew move and get behind me. He was literally pushing me.

"Just like old times," he said.

I gave Andrew a small chuckle and started to sprint when I had 200 meters left. I could not believe how fast I was running and how good I felt. I crossed the finish line, but did not need to rest. I was not even winded. I walked over to Jesus and Andrew and asked what my time was.

"Thank you for putting your trust in Me, Daniel. I know this whole experience has not been easy, but I have been with you the entire time."

"No, thank you, Jesus! I just want to make sure I am doing what you want me to do."

"Your time was 3:45. You not only broke four minutes, but you tied the world record."

"Seriously!"

"Yes, but no one will ever know. You can tell no one except for your wife. It has to be this way."

"Ah, man! I just ran the race of my life, and no one will ever know."

"You will know, and that is all that matters."

"I guess you are right, but what about the newspaper article? Won't people want to know what happened? Won't they want to know if I beat four minutes?"

"Yes, they will, so what are you going to tell them?"

"I will tell them that I never raced. I will tell them that you don't need to see to believe, and I have nothing to prove."

"That is going to be really hard on you! Are you sure you want to do that?"

"If I say I did not beat the four minutes, I may lose some believers, and if I say I broke the world record, I may lose some believers. Either way I lose! The only way to best handle this situation is to say I never ran. What do you think I should do Jesus?"

"I think you have grown even more than expected. Now, I bet you have a lot of questions for me?"

"Yes, I do! May I ask them now?"

"Sure, what would you like to know?"

"I have so many!"

"Let's go sit down over here, and you can ask what you want."

We walked over to the bench and sat down. I would finally be able to have a conversation with Jesus. It was something I had been asking for my entire life.

# CHAPTER 19

Wow!  A conversation with Jesus, unbelievable!  How many times have I wished I could do that, and now I was going blank on all my questions?

"What would you like to know, Daniel," Jesus asked?

"I have so many questions that my mind is going blank."

"Maybe I can help you.  Just clear your mind and talk to me like you have been doing so your entire life."

"Can I start with why me?  Why was I picked to do this?"

"Sure.  I have a simple answer.  Why not you?  Are you a good person?  Are you a good husband, father, and friend?"

"I think so!"

"Then you have already answered your own question. I love everyone equally, so again, I say, "Why not you?"

"Ok, I get it. Why is there so much death in the world?"

"Boy, you get right to it don't you. This answer may be a little complicated, but simple at the same time. Without life, there can be no death, and without death, there can be no life. People have free will, and with that, they get something very important, a choice. Everyone has a choice, and we cannot interfere with free will."

"I think I understand, but you answer like Andrew does."

Jesus began to laugh at this statement and so did Andrew. They looked at each other and then laughed again.

"What is so funny," I asked?

"You! We are not laughing at you; we are laughing with you. No, I take that back, we are laughing at you. Daniel, of course, we sound alike. We spend a lot of time together.

"What is heaven like?"

"Oh, Daniel, it is too hard to explain it to you in this form.  I'll tell you what.  Please close your eyes for a moment."

I proceeded to close my eyes, and Jesus showed me what heaven was like.  I cannot even begin to put it into words, but I remember that I was smiling, laughing, and when I became aware that I was back talking to Jesus, I had tears coming down my face.

"How was that, Daniel?"

"Thank you, Jesus.  All I can say is thank you!"

"Do I remember heaven when I die?"

"Yes, you do!  Everything that Andrew told you about family and how you find them when you are down here is correct."

"Do bad people go to heaven?"

"Anyone that wants to enter into my Fathers' kingdom may enter."

"Do angels appear when I die?"

"Yes, you are never alone.  Your old friends and family are waiting for you.  Your last breath here is your first breath in heaven. You will hear that many people actually see and talk to their deceased loved ones. They can see both worlds when they are near death. Usually, the last two people they call for are their mother and father."

"Do angels hear our prayers?"

"Yes, when you pray, an angel is eager to listen, and they are running around happy to help."

"How do people I know appear in heaven? My grandfather was sick and lost a lot of weight before he died."

"Everyone is perfect and in perfect form."

"I am having a hard time getting over the death of a loved one. I miss people when they die. Does that pain I am feeling ever go away?"

"Daniel, unfortunately, the pain never goes away. You will never get over losing a loved one, but you will learn to adjust to a life without them. Although they are home with us, you are still here mourning, and it is natural to feel the way you do. Everything will just be different! Remember, a life may have ended, but the relationship has not."

"Can they hear me when I talk to them?"

"Yes! Even though you cannot hear them, they definitely hear you, and sometimes find different ways to communicate."

"How?"

"Maybe a song, a dream, a smell, or anything that helps you to remember them. Many people just write this off as a coincidence. If they really learned to listen, and search their heart, they would know it is true."

"How do you look at suicide? What if I want to get to heaven now?"

"Daniel, we cannot control free will and this is a tough question. I will try to answer so you can understand. In essence, you go to the end of the line."

"The end of the line?"

"To come back to learn more lessons."

"Am I doing all I can? Am I living my life the way you want me to?"

"Only you can answer that. You are a good man, and you put others first. You care about people, and you love them. That is all we ask of you. Love the Lord your God with all your heart and with all your soul and with all your mind. This is the first and greatest commandment. And the second is love your neighbor as yourself."

"I know I have a family on earth. Do I have a family in heaven?"

"Everyone in heaven is one big family. Whomever your family was down here is still your family in heaven. That never changes!"

"What do I remember when I go to heaven? Do I remember this life? Do I take my memories with me? Does love go with me?"

"You remember everything about your life on earth, and yes, love stays with you."

"Is there such a thing as karma?"

"Let's just say what goes around, comes around!"

"Am I judged by you when I get to heaven?"

"Yes and no! When you are first welcomed, we review your life together, and your experiences on earth. Did you learn the lessons you were sent to learn? How did you treat other people? Many people judge themselves much harder than I ever will."

"Why is there war?"

"The simple answer is because there is free will. People always have a choice. Most wars have been started because of one's opinion, differences, or religion."

"Why are there diseases like Alzheimer's, Parkinson's, and cancer?"

"Again, this is a simple answer, but complicated at the same time. Do you remember Andrew speaking to you about how some people are here for a day, some are here for a few years, and some are here much longer? Everything is decided and planned before you come down. You decide how long you are going to live, when you are going to come home, how you die, and so on. Nothing is left to chance."

"Yes, why?"

"Let's say that your son needs very specific lessons, and the only way he can get those lessons to continue his growth, is if you develop cancer. You struggle together, you learn together, you grow together because of the unique situation you are in. Down here it seems unfair, you ask why, and everyone around you may be angry. In heaven, everyone is watching, and they are impressed at the courage, passion, and dedication that is displayed to teach the lesson. Unfortunately, neither of you remember agreeing to this, but if you could see your entire purpose, you would understand. Again, this is where faith comes in. No one said it was easy, and at times, it seems too difficult to bear, but we are always with you. Even though we hate to see you struggle, it is sometimes necessary."

"I guess it is one of those things I may never understand."

"And, that is ok, Daniel!"

"Are people really taking longer to learn their lessons? Is that really why the population has grown so much?"

"That is part of it. People are losing the connection they once had with one another. We really don't talk to each other anymore. We were hoping this experiment would help people begin to change."

"Why can't you just appear and tell people that you are disappointed with them, and you want them to change?"

"Again, the choice must be their choice, and they must make it because of their faith, not because they saw me."

"I apologize for asking this, but I have always wondered. Were you married when you were on earth?"

"My turn to ask you a question before I answer that. Do you believe in me?"

"With all my heart."

"Would it matter to you or change your faith if I were married?"

"No!"

"Again, you have answered you own question. Why does it matter?"

"I don't know, I guess it doesn't. I believe you might have been married. Do I need to go to church?"

"Do you feel closer to me when you go?"

"Yes!"

"Then go to church. You do what you are comfortable with. We do not judge. People judge!"

"I remember Andrew telling me that."

"Why do you allow suffering in the world if you have the power to stop it?"

"That is a tough question. First of all, I do not allow suffering. Much of the suffering is because of free will, and the many people who need it for their growth."

"I still do not understand!"

"Sometimes, we need to see the long-term goal or big picture, and realize that our suffering is necessary to fulfill our purpose. By making it through this hardship or tough time, you get to know me in ways others do not. It brings us closer together."

"Why do bad things happen to good people?"

"Another good question Daniel! This is a very simple question, but has a complicated answer, so I will try to explain it to you so you can understand it. Bad things happen to good people because I need to prepare them for what comes next. When those people get to heaven, they are highly respected and revered by all. The more practice they get, the better they are at handling the situation. Therefore, even some of the angels look to them for guidance. Sometimes bad situations don't build character. They reveal it!"

"I have often wondered what my purpose was. Wouldn't it be easier just to tell people what their purpose is? Wouldn't they just get right to it?"

"Yes, that is part of the answer. We help guide people in finding their purpose. Along the way, they are learning about life. They are gaining invaluable insight. Many people would miss some of the most important experiences if they knew and went straight to their purpose."

Jesus made me feel at ease as we continued talking. Our conversation was going well, but then Jesus looked at me again with a look that penetrated deep into my soul and asked me a question about Him.

"Daniel, how do you think people would react if you told them you saw me?"

"I am not sure. Maybe think I am slightly crazy. Why do you ask?"

"Because when you speak at church, you are going to tell people that you not only saw me, but we had a conversation. Are you prepared to handle the consequences of that?"

"Yes, I am!"

"Even if that means people may look at you differently, or you lose your job?"

"Yes! I don't care what people think. My job is important to me, and I certainly don't want to lose it, but if it is your will, I will abide by your decision."

"Thank you for not only your unconditional love, but also your support, Daniel."

"Shouldn't I be saying that to you?"

Jesus started laughing again, and Andrew followed suit.

"Laughing at me again," I asked?

"Yep," He replied.

"Does everyone have a soul?"

"Yes! It may get confused sometimes, but everyone has a soul."

"Why do some people get special gifts like the ability to play professional sports or a beautiful singing voice?"

"Everyone on earth has special gifts. Some people just find out what their gift is earlier than others. It may not be as prominent, but it is there."

"What do I say to all the people who do not believe in you?"

"This answer may be surprising to you, but nothing."

"Nothing?"

"Nothing, because those people will not believe no matter what you say, nor are they ready to believe."

"If people are not going to believe, then what was the point of doing all of this?"

"Many people will believe, Daniel. If you can get just one person to change how they look at the world and everything in it, you have done your job."

"You did not ask me to get people to change how they look at the world. You asked me to help bring people back to God?"

"Correct, but this is all part of it. There is a master plan for everyone. Just live each day the best you can, be kind to one another, and give thanks for all that you have."

"Andrew said that you have been doing this for thousands of years. Am I the only one doing this now?"

"No, there are people all over the world doing the same thing, but in a different way."

"Does it bother you when people do not believe?"

"Yes, very much! I am here to help, but I cannot force my help onto anyone. It is like watching someone struggle to get an item off the top shelf. You want just to go over and get it for them. Imagine how hard it would be to just sit there and watch them struggle."

"What happened to the cross that you were crucified on?"

"That is an interesting question, and it is the first time anyone ever asked that before.  It is in a safe place."

"What do I do after this?"

"What do you mean?"

"I mean do I continue to tell people about my experiences and all that happened for the rest of my life?"

"Yes, people will eventually forget and continue on with their day to day living.  They will get busy again and slowly, slowly, put us off to the side until they need something.  Those that truly believe will always believe, and those that you have helped to believe will also believe.  We will do that same thing in a hundred years or so, maybe even sooner if everyone continues on the way that they are."

"Thank you, Jesus, thank you for everything.  Thank you for all that I have, my family, my health, their health, and all the blessings you provide on a daily basis."

"You have done well, Daniel, and you realize something very important. Gratitude! You are constantly praying and giving thanks for all that you have."

"Is that wrong? I heard we should only say a prayer once because praying for the same thing over and over again may make you angry."

"Do you ever have to ask you kids to help out around the house more than once?"

"All the time!"

"Does it change the way you feel about them?"

"No, but it annoys me sometimes."

"Daniel, you pray as often as you like and as many times as you like. I will never turn anyone away. Do you have any other questions you would like to ask me?"

"I am sure I do, but I cannot think of them right now."

"You can always ask them later, and Daniel?"

"Yes, Jesus?"

"Please, remember that I am always with you, I will always listen, and I love you and all mankind."

Jesus then put His hand on my head, gave me a blessing, and turned to walk away with Andrew.

"Wait!" I screamed. "Jesus?"

"Yes, Daniel?"

"I forgot to say I love you too!"

Jesus began to laugh at this statement and so did Andrew. They looked at each other, shook their heads, and then laughed again. I watched as they slowly disappeared into the sunlight. I sat there for a little while to collect my thoughts, and go over what had just happened. I thought to myself that I had to be the luckiest man on earth, and committed at that moment to making sure I got the message out to everyone I could.

## Chapter 20

I could not sleep and kept thinking about everything that had happened over the last few months. What an unbelievable story! I finally got out of bed and went into the den. I called for Andrew, and he appeared.

"Hello, Daniel!"

"Hello, Andrew. I have so much on my mind that I don't know where to start. I know I have one last assignment left, and that is to speak at my church, but why my church, and how many people am I really going to reach?"

"You will speak at your church because it is your church. Remember, Daniel, your kindness can be infectious and have a snowball effect. If you can change a few people, and they can change a few people, pretty soon, you start making a difference. Our goal was to get people to turn back to God. At least you are making people reevaluate how they see Him. Then free will comes back into play."

"I just want to make sure I am doing what I am supposed to be doing."

"Daniel, you have done well, and we are very proud of you. It may not show now, but you will begin to see the change. Remember, there are some things that you will not understand, but this is where your faith comes in."

"I know, Andrew. I trust you one hundred percent, and I know that everything happens for a reason. Thank you again for everything."

"You sound like you are saying goodbye!"

"No, I know you are always with me, and I am so thankful for everything."

"No, thank you for all your work and more importantly, for believing."

"It has been my honor."

"Unfortunately, Daniel, you are going to have to write the speech yourself. Just look deep inside and speak from the heart. You can never go wrong with that."

"Ok, Andrew, I just hope I say the right things."

"Trust yourself, trust the Lord, and row to shore."

"I am sorry, what did you say?"

"It is an old Russian proverb, Daniel. It means trust in God that He will do things for you, but you still have the responsibility to do things for Him."

"Oh, I get it! I will start writing as soon as you leave."

"Well, goodnight then!"

Andrew then disappeared, and I began to write what I was going to say at church. It was weird because I was able to think very clearly and write without hesitation. It was almost like the words were being fed to me, but I know Andrew said I would have to write it by myself. Maybe they were always there, but just deeper than I thought. Once I finished, I headed up to bed to get some sleep. Before I knew it, we were in the car heading to church. During the homily, Father Smith told everyone that he was going to do something he had not done in thirty years. He was going to let a guest speaker come and talk to the congregation during mass.

"Today, we have a very special guest. He has a story to tell, and I will let him tell it. Please welcome, Daniel Lavenok!"

I stood up from the pew I was sitting in, gave a look to Mandy and the kids, and walked to the front of the church.    Andrew was standing near the steps and whispered in my mind good luck.    I walked over to Father Smith and took the wireless mic, clipped it on my shirt, looked up, and asked God to help me get this right, and began to speak.

"Good morning everyone!    Thank you for giving me the opportunity to speak to you today.    I know this is not something that normally happens here, but I was asked to speak to you by both an angel as well as Jesus.    Yes, I did say Jesus.    About three months ago, I was sitting in my den doing some school work when I heard a voice.    He said his name was Andrew, and he was an angel.    Andrew then appeared to me, and we had a long conversation.    Once I got over the initial shock, he told me I had an assignment.    He wanted me to help turn people back to God because some people have lost their way.    He went on to explain that we would do it with something that relates to most people – sports.    I have played four professional sports, and did some amazing things.    Things that I could not have done without God's help.    I know the story may sound a little crazy, but it is true.    It is up to you whether or not you choose to believe it.

Do you ever wonder why you are here? What is your purpose? How is one's life defined? Is it by the amount of money you make? Is it the legacy you leave behind? Is it by how successful you are? Who determines what that success is?

I have often wondered what my purpose in life was. I also wondered who do I want to be, not necessarily what do I want to be. When I was younger, I wanted to be a star athlete. I had dreams of hitting that last home run or making the winning shot in a big game. All of these things were great at the time, but as I grew older, my perspective on life changed. Now, who I want to be is a good husband, father, co-worker, and friend. This is the legacy I want to leave behind. I would much rather have someone say, "Wow! I remember him as being a great father who always put his family first." This would be much better than, "Wow! I remember what a great athlete he was."

After thinking about this for the longest time and calling to mind several of the books that I have read, I decided that if I really wanted my life to change, I would have to begin with myself. After all, I had to be completely honest with myself and that is not easy to do, but once I did that, everything began to fall into place. The question is, how honest can you be with yourself? I have also learned a lot about people. I have learned that all any of us really want are basically four things. We just want to fit in or be accepted, have people trust us, have someone believe in us, and to love and be loved. Yes, no one is perfect, and we all make mistakes, but that is how we learn. We all fail in life, but that does not necessarily mean we are failures. The potential to be great is inside each of us. It is a matter of tapping that potential or learning how to release it. This leads me to what I always tell my students. I am more afraid of my kids setting their expectations too low and achieving that expectation than I am of them setting their expectations too high and failing.

Where has all the compassion gone? Are you a person who would rather turn his or her back or extend your hand? When did we become so impatient with one another? Are we too scattered and busy that we forget to treat each other with dignity and respect? What is integrity? Does it even exist anymore? I believe integrity means following your moral or ethical convictions. It is doing the right thing, even when nobody is watching, or worrying about the consequences. It is honoring your word. People who have integrity are honest with God, themselves, and others. It is what we do, what we say, and what we say we do. We are identified and defined by our word, our integrity. It makes us who we are. Jesus displayed integrity. It was the essence of His being, and it identified Him. He did what was right even when no one was looking. He even died doing what He thought was right. He died for us! He showed compassion for everyone. He was patient and treated everyone He met with dignity and respect. Why can't we use His example on a daily basis? Are we really so busy that we have forgotten that we are here to help one another? I want to honor Jesus, and I will do whatever I need to do in order to do that, but that is me. I am not asking you to do the same. That is up to you.

People are always asking what God is going to do for them. Instead, why not ask what God is going to do through them. God has a purpose, and man has a purpose, however, they may not be the same. Stop trying to figure everything out and just believe in Him. We have all heard that life is about the journey, not just the destination. Live your life so that when you are gone, you leave something for people to remember. You are in control of your own destiny! Let me ask you a few questions. How many of you have children? When they come home, do you ask them how school was? I am sure you do. Do you ask them about their tests and quizzes? Do you ask about their grades? That just shows that you care, and are involved in their life. Please listen to this next question carefully. Do you ever ask them what they did to help someone, or what they did to make someone smile? I ask this, not to upset you, but rather to shift your focus and change your thinking. Why does worth always have to be associated with a number? To be successful, many people feel they need to continue to climb some kind of corporate ladder, but what if that ladder is resting against the wrong wall? Also, be careful who you choose to associate your time with because they won't be with you when you stand before God.

Jesus asked me to use my wedding analogy. He did not say it was right or wrong, but wanted me to share it anyway. I know many of you have been to a wedding. The hall is all decorated, and the room is laid out with a head table, and then all the other tables. The bride and groom and the wedding party usually sit at the head table, and then the closest family members sit up front. I have been to some weddings where my wife and I sat in the back by the kitchen. We heard the dishes clanging, watched the doors swing open and close, and was served pretty close to last. It was very hard to see everything that was going on. I believe, and this is just me saying this, but I believe when you are in heaven, it is the same way. I don't want to sit at the back of the biggest party of them all. I am not worthy to sit at the head table, but I would like to sit as close to the front as possible. Every time I do something nice for someone, I move up a table. At least that is my belief.

I know I am asking you to believe what I am saying without any proof. I also know that many of you may think I am crazy or am doing this for some kind of publicity stunt. I assure you, I am not. I want you to know that Jesus loves you. How do I know this? Because He told me He does when I talked to Him. He also reminded me that things come to us not when we want them, but when we are ready. He reminded me to tell everyone to look around. Just open your eyes and really look. You can always find someone that is in need of help. Maybe you are already doing that. If you are, thank you. I know He appreciates it. Remember, God made human beings to dream together and inspire one another. When God says no, do not look at it as He is rejecting, maybe He is redirecting instead. Life is not fair, but God is. God heals pain, He does not cause it. God loves, He does not hate. Don't blame God for the things you did not get, instead, thank God for the things you have. Your time here is short! We need to make the best of it and recognize what we are truly here for, to help and serve others. Jesus did, and He wants us to do the same.

After I finished speaking, I handed the microphone back to Father Smith and sat down next to Mandy.

"Nice job! If anything, you made people think," Mandy said.

I thought about what she had said for the rest of mass. Did I really make people think? Did I do what Andrew had originally asked me to do? Would people really start to turn back to God because of what I had done? Only time would tell.

CHAPTER 21

It was about 4:00 a.m. when I woke up. I could not shut my mind off with everything that had happened. I went downstairs to make some hot chocolate and called for Andrew.

"Hello, Daniel," he said.

"Hello, Andrew."

"Couldn't sleep?"

"No, not really. I guess I could not shut my mind off. This is a lot to take in and process."

"I understand, Daniel. Are you concerned about something?"

"Yes and no. I think I understand what has happened, but I just worry that I did not do what I was meant to do. I actually enjoyed this whole experience and feel guilty that I was able to do what I did, while others may not have this opportunity. Is that wrong?"

"No, Daniel! It is not wrong. Remember, you were chosen for this, so you should not feel guilty. I know it is your nature, but try not to feel too bad."

"I can't help it. When you think about what I was able to do, I mean really think about it, doesn't it seem unfair?"

"Daniel, what was your original assignment?"

"You asked me to help people turn back to God."

"And you have started that process, but you may not recognize that. I keep forgetting you are human and cannot see what I see. Yesterday, there were several professional athletes that had an opportunity to go out on the town and really live it up. Many of them have more money than they know what to do with. Everyone recognizes who they are, and for the most part, their lives are pretty good. However, last night, one of the players said he did not want to go out. He would rather attend church. It is not that this never happens, but this is someone who is beginning to look at himself to see if he is really fulfilled. Yes, he could have anything he wants, but something was missing. I think he figured out it was God. Not only did he not go out, but he, as well as many other players, some of the coaching staff, wives, and children attended the mass that was provided. It was a packed house."

"So, you think that happened because of what I did?"

"Well, he brought you up in his conversation to the other players.  He wondered if any of what happened to you could be true.  People are starting to think.  They are starting to have hope, and that is one of the single greatest things anyone can have."

"That makes me feel a little better."

"Daniel, may I ask you a question?"

"Sure!"

"Besides God, what is the single most important thing in your life?"

"Oh, that is simple Andrew, my family."

"What would be next?"

"I am not sure.  Why do you ask?"

"How about I make it easy for you.  Here is a list of five things.  Just put them in order with number one being most important."

Andrew asked me to write down the following list:

1. Friends

2. Health

3. Career

4. Money

5. Integrity

"This is a tough list, Andrew, but I am pretty sure I have it figured out."

"You don't need more time?"

"No, I don't think so."

"May I have your list please?"

"Sure, integrity would be first, followed by health, friends, career, and finally money."

"Do you think that is the order most people would have?"

"I am not sure!  Is that a trick question?"

"No, I am just curious as to what you think other people would do."

"I am not sure.  I only know what I would do."

"Why would you put integrity above everything else?"

"Way back when we first started this, I told you I used to be concerned about what I wanted to be instead of who I wanted to be. When I am no longer on this earth, the only thing I leave behind are memories. My honor and integrity are really important to me."

"Another reason why you were selected."

"Andrew, may I ask you a question?"

"Sure!"

"I know you said God only gives you what you can handle, and I think I understand why bad things happen to good people, but why do a lot of people I know have a ton of issues on their plate?"

"It is necessary for their growth."

"Ok, I get that, but right now my father-in-law is battling cancer, my mother is sick, my son is having issues at school, my daughter was upset about sports, my superintendent is angry and she thinks I am hurting the district because of what I did, my mother-in-law and my brother-in-law..."

"Let me stop you right there. When did you start praying to God and ask Him for His help?"

"Right when the very first thing happened. Why?"

"Because you knew that your plate might get full, but you did not wait. Many people wait and the burden gets heavier and heavier."

"But that does not make any sense. Shouldn't my burden get easier if I asked God for help right away?"

"No, you are still going to have a lot on your plate. The difference is God will be with you to help you get through it. Remember, He wants you to lean on Him."

"I am still a little confused, Andrew. Sorry!"

"Daniel, imagine you have ten yards of mulch to move. The amount is never going to change, right?"

"Yes, I am following you."

"Now imagine that God comes to help you move it. You are still moving the ten yards, but your burden is lighter because you have help."

"When you put it that way, it is easier for me to understand. So, you are saying that life may be more difficult at times, but I know I always have God to lean on?"

"Exactly!"

"And people do not realize that, hence, our little experiment."

"Yes, Daniel. I think you finally have it now. People have changed. Times have changed. You live in a time where people are constantly questioning God's existence. All we ever wanted was for people to turn to God and know that He is real. He loves you, and He will always be there for you."

"Do you think we were able to do that?"

"I believe so, but we will have to wait and see."

"Will I ever see you again?"

"Of course! It may not be for a while, but I am never far away."

"Thank you, Andrew, for everything. I really appreciated the experience. I hope it helped do what it was supposed to do. I know I have grown and changed my way of thinking. I just hope others will follow."

"You are welcome, Daniel!"

Andrew turned around and began to walk away.

"Wait! Are you leaving?"

"Yes, Daniel. Don't worry. I am always watching."

I gave Andrew a big hug and said goodbye. He started to glow a brilliant white and slowly began to rise. He stared at me, and I felt as though his gaze went right to my soul, just like the first time we met and put a thought into my head.

"I believe we have fixed that whole in your heart. And, Daniel!"

"Yes, Andrew?"

"I want you to remember this. Just because people do not believe in God does not mean He does not believe in them."

I watched him go through the ceiling and then disappear. I knelt down and thanked God for all that I have. Then I went into the kitchen to help my wife with breakfast.

## EPILOGUE

It was about six months later when I was working on the computer checking some projects when Andrew suddenly appeared.

"Hello, Daniel! How are you?"

"I am fine Andrew. It is good to see you. Are you here to check up on our progress?"

"Unfortunately, no! I am not here for that."

"Oh, why are you here then?"

Just when Andrew was about to answer, another angel appeared.

"Did you tell him yet," he said to Andrew.

"No, not yet! Daniel, this is Michael. We are here because we need your help."

Made in the USA
Coppell, TX
05 February 2021

49754758R00125